WAKING THE DEAD

To order additional copies of *Waking the Dead,* by Russell Burrill, call **1-800-765-6955.**

Visit us at **www.reviewandherald.com** for information on other Review and Herald® products.

Other books by Russell Burrill include:
Creating Healthy Adventist Churches Through Natural Church Development
Hope When the World Falls Apart
Radical Disciples for Revolutionary Churches
Recovering an Adventist Approach to the Life and Mission of the Local Church
Rekindling a Lost Passion
Revolution in the Church
The Revolutionized Church of the 21st Century

These may be obtained at your local Adventist Book Center, or by calling **1-800-765-6955.**

WAKING THE DEAD

Returning Plateaued and
Declining Churches to Vibrancy

RUSSELL BURRILL

REVIEW AND HERALD® PUBLISHING ASSOCIATION
HAGERSTOWN, MD 21740

HART BOOKS
A Ministry of Hart Research Center
FALLBROOK, CALIFORNIA

This book was
Edited by Raymond H. Woolsey
Copyedited by Delma Miller and James Cavil
Cover designed by Leumas Design/Willie Duke
Cover photo by Getty Images
Interior designed by Candy Harvey
Electronic makeup by Shirley M. Bolivar
Typeset: 11.5/13 ITC Garamond Book

PRINTED IN U.S.A.

08 07 06 05 04   5 4 3 2 1

R&H Cataloging Service
Burrill, Russell
    Waking the dead: returning plateaued and
declining churches to vibrancy.

    1. Church growth.   I. Title.

                254.5

ISBN 0-8280-1861-8

Acknowledgments

Over the years I have had the opportunity to work with many churches, some as an outside consultant and others that I have pastored. In my ministry I have learned much that has helped me lead a church back to vibrancy. In addition, I have read extensively and learned so much from others. Some things worked; others did not. In the pages of this book I have shared that which I have learned. Many things I have gleaned from others and may not have properly footnoted it because it has become such a part of me. I wish to acknowledge my indebtedness to all those I have learned from.

A special word of thanks is extended to Alice McIntyre, my administrative assistant, for her help in making this book possible. She has painstakingly checked every reference for accuracy, as well as offered numerous suggestions to help me convey my thoughts more clearly. I also wish to thank my wife, Cynthia, for her encouragement and insights, especially in the chapters on worship. A special thanks goes to Lyle Litzenberger for sharing the detailed information from the data bank for Adventist natural church development. Without their help this book would not have been possible. I also wish to thank Dan Houghton and HART Research, along with the Review and Herald Publishing Association, for publishing this work and making it possible to help vitalize so many Adventist churches.

It is my prayer that this book will help pastors and lay leaders bring their church back to its strong mission foundations. Only then can God's work progress and ultimately be finished. May this work contribute to the hastening of the day of the Advent. Maranatha. Come, Lord Jesus.

Contents

1

Recovering Lost Love

Do you remember when you had to arrive early at church to get a seat? Do you remember when activity at the church was abundant and there was always something to do? Do you remember when baptisms occurred regularly at your church? Do you remember when your church seemed so alive with the Spirit that you just longed to be there Sabbath after Sabbath?

Is your church like that today? Or has your church dwindled to the place where most members realize that its glory days are in the past? When your church people get together, do they talk about what used to be instead of what is yet to come? When someone mentions reaching lost people, do your church members say to themselves, *Usually no one responds when we have meetings, so why try?* Has your church experienced failure after failure, to the place where the members have assumed that all the people who can be reached in your community have already been reached?

If the above scenario sparks a responsive chord in your heart, then this book is for you. In the pages of this book we will be exploring how to take a church that has either plateaued or been declining and move it into a growth cycle. The suggestions offered here will not be easy, but if a church is serious about becoming vibrant, it is possible by the grace of God to accomplish that.

Many have become discouraged with the churches that are not growing, and have opted to plant new ones. That is fine; we certainly need to continue to plant new churches, but at the same time we need to help existing churches recover their lost mission and become vibrant. Many people have gone beyond discouragement and pronounced the traditional church dead, in need only of burial. I don't believe that. God can renew His church, and He still performs miracles. Remember, Jesus raised the dead, so He can certainly raise up dead churches.

The Difficulty of the Task

The task of turning churches around is not easy. In fact, it can be very difficult. George Barna, respected researcher, in his book *Turn-Around Churches*[1] attempted to examine churches in the United States that had been turned around. He wanted to discover what caused these churches to succeed at renewal. Barna indicates that, upon examination, he could find only 30 such churches in the entire United States. This was not a large enough sample to produce accurate statistics, but he declared that 30 churches were all that could be located. Evidently churches that have changed course from decline to growth are very rare.

Barna then continues to share what he did find out about those 30 churches that moved from deterioration to regeneration. There were several common denominators. Usually it happened with the arrival of a new pastor. The new pastor immediately plunged into the work of turning the church around. It took a lot of hard work. The pastors usually put in 80-hour weeks. Barna concluded that only younger pastors should attempt to turn churches around, and that they should attempt only a single turnaround in their entire pastoral career. Why? Because the workload and the stress load were so heavy.

Reading Barna's book could make you very discouraged. You could respond by thinking, *Why try?* You might feel that it would be best just to close the door and start a new church. In some cases that may actually be the optimum solution; however, it may be that the church is worth saving. Remember, Barna is speaking about churches that are on the decline—churches that are on the plateau are easier to move into growth mode than declining churches are.

Whether your church is declining or on the plateau, there is hope. Do not be discouraged. The way may not be easy; there may be some very difficult roads ahead, but it is possible. As a pastor, through the years I have seen churches move off the plateau and into growth. One church, for example, moved from an attendance of 250-280 to one of 400-450 within a five-year time frame. It had been stuck at the 250-280 level for more than 10 years, a definite plateau, but with God's help it was able to break the barrier and grow again.

I remember another church that was on the decline. The first Sabbath I attended, there were three people present out of a membership of 30. On a good Sabbath there might be 15 in attendance, but that was unusual. Over the next four years we saw this declining church move to an attendance of 80.

Having experienced such turnarounds, I am more optimistic than George Barna appears to be in his book. It may be that Adventist churches are easier to turn around than some other Protestant churches. The reason may have to do with the fact that Seventh-day Adventists still remember when we were a vibrant movement of God. Our mission involvement is not a part of ancient history, as it is in some denominations. There is a spark in the

Adventist mind-set that inspires us to believe that God will lead the church to the accomplishment of its mission. At the core most Adventists want to see their church turn around and become a mighty instrument in the hand of God for the fulfillment of the Great Commission.

God Can Turn Around Churches

It is not unusual for churches to reach a plateau. It happened early in Christianity. Even the church of the disciples had problems assimilating new people into its fellowship. Look at the conflicts that arose over how the widows of Greek origin were being treated as compared to those of Hebrew origin. It led to some real problems in the early church (Acts 6:1). The church had to incorporate some changes if it was to continue growing and fulfilling the mission of Christ.

A few years later the church hit another crisis. This dispute centered on the question of whether one had to become a Jew in order to be a Christian; whether Christianity was a universal religion without Jewish trappings. The Jerusalem Council decided in favor of the mission of Christ for all people; they would not make the Jewish requirements a necessity for becoming a Christian (Acts 15). The result of that decision was that the church kept on growing.

If the early church had not made those changes, Christianity would ultimately have become just another sect of Judaism and not the universal religion of today. Evidently churches must continually change if they are to grow and remain relevant to the society that God is calling them to reach. The message of the church does not change, but the way it is packaged needs constant examination.

Near the end of the first century God commissioned John, an exile on the isle of Patmos, to write a letter to the seven churches in Asia Minor. That letter is called the book of Revelation. John is first directed by Christ to address the church at Ephesus, which we have seen to be representative of the first-century church. Listen again to the counsel God gave that church:

"To the angel of the church in Ephesus write: The One who holds the seven stars in His right hand, the One who walks among the seven golden lampstands, says this: 'I know your deeds and your toil and perseverance, and that you cannot endure evil men, and you put to the test those who call themselves apostles, and they are not, and you found them to be false; and you have perseverance and have endured for My name's sake, and have not grown weary. But I have this against you, that you have left your first love. Therefore remember from where you have fallen, and repent and do the deeds you did at first; or else I am coming to you and will remove your lampstand out of its place—unless you repent'" (Rev. 2:1-5).

Even the first-century church was losing its first love by the end of the first century, less than 70 years from the start of Christianity. Evidently the church in John's final days was in danger of forgetting its mission, content with what it had already accomplished and not continuing in the work of sharing Christ's message with the world. It had lost that first love.

Yet note that John's counsel from God to this church does not present it as hopeless. There was hope for a church that had lost its first love. However, it needed to repent. That repentance included remembering the point from which it had fallen. Evidently a church must look back and recall the dream that birthed it if it is to move into the future. We will talk more about this when dealing with a later church, but note the strong scriptural support for turning churches around, based on remembering the dream.

The other counsel John offers is to "do the deeds you did at first" (verse 5). Part of looking back at where the church has been is to discover what it did in the beginning. Think back to the first phase of your church, to a time when your church was very vibrant. Probably you will discover that the ministry of your church was responsive to the needs of the community. Recovery is not merely repeating the early deeds, but examining them to discover how the previous approach provided for community needs and was successful in reaching people.

Many churches make the mistake of examining the past and then attempting to replicate it. However, reproducing history rarely works, because the people in both the church and the community are different today than they were back then. Therefore, one must examine the principles that made the church successful at the start and replicate the principles in contemporary society.

Bob Logan, noted church planting specialist, while speaking at the annual SEEDS church planting conference held by the North American Division Evangelism Institute, indicated that in working with churches of various denominations he finds that the secret to their present-day problems lies in their history. He states that if a church will examine what it was like when it was a vibrant movement of God, it will find the pathway to its renewal in the present day.

So John's first-century counsel is still relevant in the twenty-first century. When you have lost your first love, you need to remember what you once were in the beginning and then do the first works. There is hope for the plateaued or declining church, but it must begin by looking back and rekindling a desire to do the first works that originally made it vibrant, by copying not the methodology but the principles that helped it focus on accomplishing the mission of Jesus.

Problem of the Last Days

Loss of first love was not only a problem of the first-century church, but was also predicted to be a major problem for God's church at the end of time. Revelation's messages are given for the actual first-century churches in those cities as well as for the church in various stages throughout its long history. Therefore, the message to the ancient church of Laodicea carries special weight for God's church in the last days. Listen again to God's message to that church.

"To the angel of the church in Laodicea write: The Amen, the faithful and true Witness, the Beginning of the creation of God, says this: 'I know your deeds, that you are neither cold nor hot; I wish that you were cold or hot. So because you are lukewarm, and neither hot nor cold, I will spit you out of My mouth. Because you say, "I am rich, and have become wealthy, and have need of nothing," and you do not know that you are wretched and miserable and poor and blind and naked, I advise you to buy from Me gold refined by fire so that you may become rich, and white garments so that you may clothe yourself, and that the shame of your nakedness will not be revealed; and eye salve to anoint your eyes so that you may see. Those whom I love, I reprove and discipline; therefore be zealous and repent. Behold, I stand at the door and knock; if anyone hears My voice and opens the door, I will come in to him and will dine with him, and he with Me. He who overcomes, I will grant to him to sit down with Me on My throne, as I also overcame and sat down with My Father on His throne. He who has an ear, let him hear what the Spirit says to the churches'" (Rev. 3:14-22).

The disease of Laodiceanism or lukewarmness is very similar to the disease of having lost one's first love. In both cases the fire and zeal of the first experience with

Jesus has grown dim and the need is great for a refreshing from the Spirit. It is easy to apply these texts personally—an individual loss of first love and lukewarmness. However, the warning is deeper. If the disease is prevalent in enough church members, then the disastrous result is that the church itself reflects lukewarmness and loss of first love.

This seems to be the condition John describes in both Ephesus and Laodicea. The whole church had turned inward and failed to reach out to others and extend the borders of the gospel. The remedy for Ephesus was to remember what they did at the beginning when they were relevant. The remedy for Laodicea was to let Jesus once again be their inspiration, as He was at the start. Putting the two together, we discover that the remedy for plateaued and declining churches is a new walk with Jesus that reexamines the dreams and vibrancy of the early days and recaptures the essence of what it means to be the church of Jesus.

So as we begin this adventure of learning how to renew plateaued and declining churches, let us remember the need of rekindling the first love and recapturing the vibrancy reflected in those who have a deep personal relationship with the living Christ. One cannot know Jesus deeply and not be empowered to accomplish His mission. In fact, to be uninvolved in the mission of the redeeming Christ reveals that He is not known at all, for mission is at the heart of what it means to be Jesus' disciple. As Ellen White has declared: "Every true disciple is born into the kingdom of God as a missionary."[2]

False Teachers

There is one other problem that causes churches to lose their way and plateau or decline. This obstacle has some very serious consequences, and a church that becomes afflicted with it is rarely rejuvenated. This problem virtually destroys churches. I have never seen a church that has experienced this problem turn around. Of course, God can always perform a miracle, but in this type of case it is rare. I refer to the disease of false teachers.

Paul was very concerned about the deadliness of this problem and warned the first-century church about the dangers of false teachers. It is amazing that within 30 years of the death of Jesus, false teachers were already rampant in the church. It seems that this has been a real problem for the church down through the centuries, so we should not be surprised to find it still happening now.

Listen to Paul's warning: "Be on guard for yourselves and for all the flock, among which the Holy Spirit has made you overseers, to shepherd the church of God which He purchased with His own blood.

"I know that after my departure savage wolves will come in among you, not sparing the flock; and from among your own selves men will arise, speaking per-verse things, to draw away the disciples after them. Therefore be on the alert, remembering that night and day for a period of three years I did not cease to admon-ish each one with tears. And now I commend you to God and to the word of His grace, which is able to build you up and to give you the inheritance among all those who are sanctified" (Acts 20:29-32).

Paul's counsel here seems to be preventative rather than offering suggestions of what to do after it happens. This may be because there is so little hope to turn a church around after false teachers destroy it. Therefore, he vigorously encourages churches to make certain that false teachers do not come in and tear down the flock that God has created.

In Adventism I have noticed several churches that have been enveloped in false teachings of one kind or another. It is not one specific teaching that ruins the church. Anything that distracts from the foundations of our faith saps the church's energy and prevents it from accomplishing its mission. The result is plateau, decline, and death.

I remember one church in which the local conference invited me to hold an evangelistic series. When I met with the church board to plan the series, they told me that the conference wanted them to hold meetings but that they did not believe in evangelism.

Of course, they did not realize what they were saying, because declaring disbelief in evangelism is the same as declaring that you are disobedient to Jesus and His great commission. Any church that is staunchly disobedient to the Great Commission could not be construed as being a Christian church; therefore, the church was virtually declaring that it had ceased to be a Christian organization.

I responded to this church board by asking them why they didn't believe in evangelism. Their response was that they believed evangelism was delaying the Lord's return. I thought I had heard everything, but this was the most extreme case of false theology I had ever heard, so I asked them to explain how they had arrived at that belief. They informed me that every new person I brought into the church would be one more person who would have to be perfected before Jesus could come and that they had already been perfected, so they didn't want any imperfect people coming in to ruin their perfect church.

In seven years this church had gone from an attendance of 200 to one of only 20; however, the people rejoiced that the tares had been weeded out and that the righteous remained. In reality, their pompous disobedience to Jesus was almost blasphemous, and fully revealed the falseness of their claims. The tragedy was that they were lost and didn't know it. They themselves were in drastic need of evangelization.

This is an example of false teachers destroying a church. It is rare that this type of church could ever recover. The only remedy is to close the doors. It has completely abandoned the faith. This type of church comes closest to being impossible to turn around. Perhaps this is the reason that Paul warned against allowing this to happen. When a church loses its first love and becomes lukewarm, God provides a remedy, but for false teachers the Bible provides no such solution.

Why do such things happen to God's church? Why don't churches keep on growing and staying healthy year after year? The answer is that we are embroiled in the great controversy between God and Satan. Satan does not want God's church to prosper, so he studies every means possible to prevent the church from accomplishing the purpose of Jesus. There is also a human element in this problem that we will examine in chapter 3, but first we need to understand the purpose of the church clearly.

---

[1] George Barna, *Turn-Around Churches* (Ventura, Calif.: Regal Books, 1993).

[2] Ellen G. White, *The Desire of Ages* (Mountain View, Calif.: Pacific Press Pub. Assn., 1898), p. 195.

2

Recapturing the Mission

When churches are afflicted with the disease of lukewarmness or the loss of first love, the first step in recovery is to remember the passion that was felt before the falling away occurred. Jesus continually reminded the first-century church to reconsider their first works after they had initially heard the gospel. Most of us who are converts to Christ and the church remember well the enthusiasm and excitement we felt when we first learned this glorious message of hope. We wanted to share it with everyone.

I remember as a late teenager joining a small church of 25 members in a city of 50,000 people. A large city of 100,000 people just 10 miles away had been completely untouched with the Advent message. Here were these people in possession of this amazing message, and they were not doing anything to reach that population for Christ. At least that is what I thought with my first-love eyes. So, being an assertive teenager, I began prodding them to do more.

It wasn't long until a dear old saint approached me, put his arm around me, and said, "Son, you have your first-love experience, and that is wonderful, but you just wait a bit, and you will lose it like the rest of us." I suddenly went from euphoria over this message to the realization that I had joined Laodicea.

It should not be normal to lose one's first love. Love for Jesus and a desire to share His message of hope should increase, not decrease, the longer we walk the Christian pathway. The deterioration of first love is always associated with the loss of a vision for reaching the lost. Jesus counsels His church to recapture the first love. That is why it is so essential for a church that has lost its first love and is afflicted with Laodiceanism to regain a sense of mission. It needs to remember the first works—to become involved once again in the mission of the redeeming Christ. By the way, involvement in mission is also an excellent antidote for false teachers. False teachers do not destroy a church so easily when it is involved in reaching lost people.

What is that mission? The marching orders of the church are clear; they come straight from the founder of Christianity. Jesus established the church on the Great Commission. Listen once again to these commanding words from our Lord as He ended His ministry and left the church in the hands of the chosen eleven.

"But the eleven disciples proceeded to Galilee, to the mountain which Jesus had designated. And when they saw Him, they worshiped Him, but some were doubtful. And Jesus came up and spoke to them, saying, 'All authority has been given to Me in heaven and on earth. Go therefore and make disciples of all the nations, baptizing them in the name of the Father and the Son and the Holy Spirit, teaching them to observe all that I commanded you; and lo, I am with you always, even to the end of the age' " (Matt. 28:16-20).

With these words Jesus established His church. It was not to be a babysitting operation. It was to be a mission agency. The reason for the existence of the church was to go forth and make disciples among all people groups. This message comes to us in the authority of the risen Lord. Jesus declares that He possesses all authority in heaven and on earth. You can't get any more authority than that. Jesus is proclaiming that He is the "CEO" of the universe. He is not asking us to go—He is telling us we must go. We have no choice. If we are His disciples, we will obey and go.

Involvement in mission is not an option for a church that is loyal to Jesus. Failure to go forth and make disciples puts a church in direct disobedience to the risen Lord, an untenable position for any church claiming to represent Christ. There is no stronger command given in Scripture than this one. This is the only place Jesus tells us to go in His authority.

Any church that is disobedient to this commission is in dereliction of its duty to the commander in chief. In religious terms, we call disobedience sin. Thus any church not involved in the mission of Jesus is virtually living in sin. When Jesus tells us to remember "from where [we] have fallen" (Rev. 2:5), we are forced back to these parting words of Jesus to His church. We must go and make disciples. This is our mission.

Many churches get involved in good projects, and people feel good about doing them, but if those projects are not helping the church fulfill Christ's commission, then they are only camouflaging disobedience to Christ. Many of these projects can be good in themselves and even be part of helping a church fulfill the Great Commission, but if they become an end in themselves, then they become a hindrance to fulfilling the mission of Christ.

For example, witnessing is a vital part of helping a church to fulfill the Great Commission. Yet the ultimate mission of the church is not only to witness but also to make disciples. If all a church does is witness but that

witness does not result in people accepting Jesus and becoming His disciples, the witness is a failure. This is not
to say that witnessing is not important. It is a vital part of
the process of disciple-making. The problem occurs
when the end product becomes the witness rather than
the making of disciples.

At the core of renewing a church is helping the
church discover, again, that it is a disciple-making organization. It is not a church with a mission—the church is
living in mission. The only pathway to recovery for a
plateaued or declining church is through a rediscovering
of the first love—a love for making disciples who will be
ready to meet Jesus when He comes. This must be at the
center of any effort to renew a dead church. There must
be a recapturing of the mission of the church.

This mission legacy was so essential for the church
that Jesus embedded it in the "DNA" of the church He established. It was so deeply entwined in their thinking that
each of the Synoptic Gospel writers included these final
mission words of Jesus in their account of the last words
of Jesus. Note Mark's account of the Great Commission:

"And He said to them, 'Go into all the world and
preach the gospel to all creation. He who has believed
and has been baptized shall be saved; but he who has dis-
believed shall be condemned. These signs will accompany those who have believed: in My name they will cast
out demons, they will speak with new tongues; they will
pick up serpents, and if they drink any deadly poison, it
will not hurt them; they will lay hands on the sick, and
they will recover.' So then, when the Lord Jesus had spoken to them, He was received up into heaven and sat
down at the right hand of God. And they went out and
preached everywhere, while the Lord worked with
them, and confirmed the word by the signs that fol-
lowed" (Mark 16:15-20).

Mark gives the same basic commission as Matthew does. Jesus ended His ministry on earth by establishing a church to accomplish His mission: making disciples. While Matthew quotes Jesus as having all authority in heaven and on earth, Mark records that Jesus sends His disciples in that authority. Therefore signs, wonders, and miracles accompany the believers as they go about the mission.

Notice again that it is not signs and miracles for the sake of the saved, but for the sake of the unsaved, so that they will recognize the authoritative power of God in the witness of God's church. Jesus wants the church to give His message with power and great authority. This is the mission of the church. It is not just to tell; it is to tell with His authority.

Luke follows in the path of Matthew and Mark in both accounts of Jesus' final words in Luke and Acts:

"And He said to them, 'Thus it is written, that the Christ would suffer and rise again from the dead the third day, and that repentance for forgiveness of sins would be proclaimed in His name to all the nations, beginning from Jerusalem. You are witnesses of these things. And behold, I am sending forth the promise of my Father upon you; but you are to stay in the city until you are clothed with power from on high'" (Luke 24:46-49).

"Gathering them together, He commanded them not to leave Jerusalem, but to wait for what the Father had promised, 'Which,' He said, 'you heard of from Me; for John baptized with water, but you will be baptized with the Holy Spirit not many days from now.' So when they had come together, they were asking Him, saying, 'Lord, is it at this time You are restoring the kingdom to Israel?' He said to them, 'It is not for you to know times or epochs which the Father has fixed by His own authority; but you will receive power when the Holy Spirit has come upon you; and you will be My witnesses both in Jerusalem, and in all Judea and Samaria, and even to the remotest part of the earth'" (Acts 1:4-8).

Luke continues the same emphasis of Matthew and Mark. The church was to go forth to be a mission agency. And for the accomplishment of that mission, Jesus promised to empower the church with the Holy Spirit. The church has been asked to witness not in human power but by the divine authority and power of the third person of the Trinity. Make no mistake. The mission is clear. There can be no detour from what Christ has commissioned, or we will be living in direct disobedience to the King of the universe. We are not a church for ourselves; we are a church for the fulfillment of the mission of Jesus.

Many Adventists pray regularly for the outpouring of the Holy Spirit. Even in declining and plateaued churches, members will earnestly beseech Jesus to send the Spirit, and then refuse to go forth for Him and make disciples. To pray for the outpouring of the Spirit yet refuse to be involved in the mission of Christ is a contradiction.

We long for the outpouring of the Spirit in latter-rain power. However, the latter rain will be like the former rain at Pentecost. What happened at Pentecost? The Holy Spirit descended, and there was a great outpouring of spiritual gifts. What will happen in the latter rain? There will also be a great outpouring of the Holy Spirit resulting in increased spiritual gifts, but if we are not using the gifts God has already given us for accomplishing His mission, why would He ever give us the latter rain and bless us with more gifts?

Others look forward to the outpouring of the Spirit in latter-rain power and assume that we must wait until then to receive the Holy Spirit's power. These people seem to believe that only then can the people in their community come to Christ. Since the latter rain is not yet falling, they hold back and don't witness. However, one must remember that in Palestine the early rains came in the fall, and the latter rains in the spring. The time in between was known as the rainy season. If we follow the analogy all the way through, we are bound to conclude that while there is a superabundance of the Holy Spirit poured out in the early and latter rains, we today are living in the rainy season of the Holy Spirit. The church does not need to wait until some future time to possess the Spirit—it can possess the Spirit right now.

Recovering the sense of mission in the church enables the church once again to pray for the Holy Spirit's power. And He will respond. God will not pour out His Holy Spirit on people who are not involved in Jesus' mission. The whole purpose of the giving of the Spirit to the church was to enable the church to fulfill the mission of Christ. Therefore, as a church recovers its mission and becomes involved in making disciples and reaching lost people, it will quickly sense new power—the power of the Holy Spirit.

The Result of No Mission

When the loss of first love, lukewarmness, or false teachers take control of a church, they paralyze it and prevent it from accomplishing its mission. All of these conditions cause a church to turn inward. With time spent waiting upon itself, the church's spiritual energy is drained by self-care that does not provide true care. The result is a church drained of the energy the Holy Spirit wants to give it.

There is a definite connection between involvement in mission and spirituality. The commitment to mission is many times a good indicator of where a church is spiritually. When a church is uninvolved in mission, it is usually in a weak spiritual condition, for a spiritually alive church finds it impossible to be indifferent to the mission of Jesus. That's why churches that are plateaued and declining need to be of great concern to us, for these problems indicate that the church is in poor spiritual condition.

Which comes first, solving the spiritual problem of the church or getting the church involved once again in mission? Through the years I have watched pastors approach this subject both ways. I remember one well-respected pastor whose philosophy of ministry was to preach great sermons. And he was a great preacher. He told me that his people were being so well fed by his sermons that they would soon grow spiritually and then become involved in mission and reaching people for Jesus. Yet after years of listening to his preaching, there was no increase in mission involvement in his church.

Nurture for the sake of nurture creates religious weaklings.* If you try to solve the spiritual problem first, you will never solve the whole problem, because people are spiritually renewed only as they go about the mission of Jesus. When people are involved in helping other people, they grow spiritually. For example, the Sabbath school teacher always gets more out of the lesson than the students do.

In attempting to turn around one plateaued church that I pastored, I found myself in a very difficult situation. I was a young pastor, and the church was notorious for infighting. Board meetings were despicable. Members would argue and fight with unkind words until decent members hated to go to the monthly board meetings.

When I arrived at the church I soon learned of the worst fight that had ever occurred in the board meeting. As the members were engaged in their usual bickering with each other, one of the members pushed the person beside him. Soon an actual fistfight broke out at the board meeting. One dear old saint rushed to the phone and dialed 911, fearing that someone would be hurt. Soon the police arrived to break up the fight at the monthly Seventh-day Adventist church board meeting.

Was this church growing? No. Were people being won to Christ through their ministry in their community? No. Would you want to bring new people into such a church? No. Should you attempt to solve the fighting problem first and then get them involved in mission? No.

As I began working among them I started to help them share their faith with others. Amazingly, as they became involved in sharing their faith the fighting slowly stopped. Church board meetings became pleasant as members started sharing stories about people being won to Jesus. The church started growing again. I learned that one must first solve the mission problem, and then it is much easier to solve the nurture problem. If I had attempted to focus on the problems, the church would have probably continued to fight. By concentrating on solving the mission problem first, the fighting problem almost solved itself.

This does not mean that you should ignore the nurture problem—the fighting needed attention. My point is that if you concentrate on just solving the nurture problem, it won't happen. You have to focus on the mission problem at the same time. There is something about being involved in the mission of Jesus that causes a church to begin to renew itself and solve its spiritual problem.

Here is the situation: A church is in spiritual trouble. Any church not growing is in spiritual trouble. What do you do? Don't concentrate on the spiritual problem. Help the church become involved in mission, and the spiritual problem will also be solved.

The church is a mission agency involved in the mission of Jesus. The devil seeks to get the church involved in side issues, fighting unnecessary battles, all in an attempt to divert the church from accomplishing the mission of Jesus. Satan does not want the church to fulfill the mission of Christ, for then his kingdom will decline as people come to Jesus.

Therefore, the spiritual battle must be fought. People must be won to Jesus. Nothing must be allowed to divert the church from the accomplishment of the mission of Jesus. Don't be fooled by Satan's subtle attempts to get the church focused on something other than its mission. Involvement in mission is the best avenue to the renewal of existing churches. In fact, a strong case could be made for the statement "There can be no renewal of the church without a corresponding involvement in mission."

As you contemplate how to bring spiritual renewal to your church, consider how you might reawaken a passion for the mission of Jesus, who left heaven and died on Calvary for the sake of reaching lost people. If Christ's mission meant so much to Him that He endured the cross, can't we make the recovery of mission the heart and center of the call to renewal?

---

* Ellen G. White, *Testimonies for the Church* (Mountain View, Calif.: Pacific Press Pub. Assn., 1948), vol. 7, p. 18.

3

The Life Cycle of Churches

First church was planted more than 50 years ago. For years it was the premier Adventist church in the area. With a membership of more than 500, it usually received an excellent pastor, who was a gifted speaker and continually led the church forward. However, as time moved on, the neighborhood surrounding the church began to change. New kinds of people moved in, many of whom did not speak the same language as those attending First church. At first there was no problem. As people moved out of the area, they still continued to come in every Sabbath for church and then retreat to the suburbs for the rest of the week, so attendance remained stable.

But after a few years some members became tired of the weekly commute and began to attend Adventist churches that were closer to them. Slowly the attendance at First church began to slide. The church held numerous evangelistic meetings, but few people were baptized. It was too difficult for members to bring their friends from the suburbs all the way in to First church each night for the meetings, and it was difficult for them to attend as well. In addition, the people in the neighborhood would not come, because they didn't speak the same language. First church had begun to die.

We call this the "life cycle." It happens to all living things. There is a period of birth, growth, maturity, decline, and eventual death. It is part of living in a sinful world. We have no trouble accepting this cycle, for it is part of what we experience in life. Yet many have failed to see that the same thing happens to churches. Churches, as living organisms, go through the same life cycle as human beings. In fact, the average life span of a church is just about the same as the human life span, about 70 years.

Of course, a few churches will live beyond their threescore and ten, just as some people do, but 70 appears to be the average. Needless to say, some churches don't even make it to 70. The reason so many churches are caught in the plateau and declining stages is that they have reached the appropriate age. Interestingly, just as people who have become sick and feeble because of a poor lifestyle can be rejuvenated through a healthy diet and a good exercise program, so can some churches. It is possible for older churches to regain some of their vibrancy, but it will require radical action for that to happen. Just as there is a price to pay for people to regain their health, so churches must be willing to pay the price to move away from the pit of death. Actually, most churches will reach their plateau by the time they are only 15 years of age, which is about when most humans stop growing.

It appears that churches mimic human life in other ways. Evidently, when a church is planted, it takes on the characteristics of the generation that planted it. As time continues, fewer and fewer people relate to the values of that generation. Even though the original planters have left, the church continues in the tradition of the values instilled by the founders directly into its DNA. As fewer people relate to those values, the church slowly loses touch with the world around it. The result is decay and decline. After 70 years there are so few people who relate to those values that the church closes its doors.

Does this have to happen? No, but a church has to be willing to continue to adapt to its surroundings by relating to the culture that surrounds the church. If a church doesn't adapt, it ultimately becomes like the Amish, who have done well to preserve the heritage of the past but no longer relate to the contemporary world. The world then relates to them as an oddity, a museum of how life used to be. A church in this situation ceases to have any influence on the world around it. This must never describe the church of Jesus.

Research has revealed that the older a congregation becomes, the more difficult it is for that congregation to reach new people. Adventist researcher Roger Dudley discovered that young churches contain more new Christians:

"Churches where most members have been in the church for twenty or more years are not growing. Growing churches have a great proportion of their memberships made up of recent converts. . . . New converts are the best potential soul winners because they still have many contacts with non-church members. . . . And often the new convert in his first love will be more active in telling his friends what the Lord has done for him." [1]

This research has been substantiated by the wider Christian community. Researchers have discovered that younger churches have more baptisms per member than older congregations do.

"If baptism rates per 100 resident members are used as a measure of efficiency for a church, then young churches are more efficient than old churches. The older a church gets, the less efficient it is in baptizing new converts." [2]

This extensive study revealed that churches under 11 years of age averaged 9.5 baptisms for every 100 resident members, whereas churches more than 41 years of age averaged only 3.7 baptisms.[3]

This is one of the compelling reasons that church planting is so necessary. If a denomination does not continually plant new churches, the denomination will soon die because of the life cycle. However, in order to have the kind of growth needed to finish the work of God we must not only plant churches; we must also seek to practice some radical surgery to turn existing churches around and extend their productive life. I am not talking about life support, but vibrancy. Churches that have moved out of the growth mode and into the plateau and declining mode need some serious attention in order to make them vibrant churches for Jesus.

Stages of a Life Cycle

There are five basic stages in the life cycle of churches. Some authors would add additional stages, but they are usually only a breakdown of these five basic stages: birth, growth, maturity, decline, and death. The first step in recovery for a church is to identify the stage it is in. Only then can the church realize where it is headed and identify the steps that should be taken in order to bring it to renewal. As we describe each of the stages, begin to think which stage best represents your church.

The first stage of the life cycle is birth. It is quite easy to identify this stage, for it directly follows the planting of the church. In this stage there is excitement in the air. New ideas are quickly picked up and implemented as the church revels in the newness of life. The church is usually meeting in rented quarters, and members are willing to come early and help set things up for church each Sabbath.

The church is strongly committed to accomplishing

its mission. It desperately needs new people. Its resources are being poured into reaching people, and the members willingly sacrifice so that this can happen. The church was started for the purpose of reaching lost people for the kingdom of God. Very little time is taken up in committees, and organization is very limited. Most of the members are engaged in working for Christ. Morale is very high, and excitement builds in anticipation of what God is going to do through this new congregation. Ideas are tried; if they don't work, they are quickly discarded and other methods are tried. Change happens very quickly, and there is little resistance to new ideas.

The second stage of the life cycle is growth. In this stage the church begins to expand in response to all the activity that takes place in stage 1. New members are baptized, and the church starts growing at a regular pace year by year. It is an exciting place to be as new people are added to the family of God. Mission continues to have wide support in the church, and members are highly committed to it.

In response to all that the church is doing, a structure is developed that will enable it to fulfill its mission. New organizations and groups are quickly established in response to the needs the church sees in the surrounding community. As the church sees people coming to faith in Christ, morale builds. The church feels good about itself. Members are proud of what God is accomplishing through their church. The church is still able to adapt to new situations and make changes as needed, but fewer changes seem necessary as the church experiences continued success in its ministry.

The third stage in the life cycle is the time of maturity. Growth has begun to decline, but the vitality remains. The church has leveled off to a certain number of people, and the members feel satisfied with what they have accomplished. They begin to relax and enjoy the fruits of their labor. They are still involved in mission to some degree. They make certain that they take in as many members as they lose by death, transfer, or inactivity. The result is that the church cycle develops a plateau. Everything appears to be going well for the church. There are enough people to fulfill all the major programs of the church.

Life has become comfortable for the church. Yet the seeds of death have already been sown. To suggest to this church that it is headed downhill would be an insult. They would point immediately to all the successes they are experiencing. "Numbers aren't everything," they say, but they have ceased to experience continual growth. "After all, why should we keep reaching out when our sanctuary is already full each Sabbath? We have arrived, and we want to enjoy it."

The fourth stage of the life cycle is the period of decline. The church may enter this stage even before it begins to experience numerical decline. The state of decline is more an attitude than anything else. Mission has ceased to be the driving force of the congregation. They give lip service to it, but few people in the congregation could articulate the mission or vision of the church if they were asked. New members simply feel they have joined a nice church, but they have no concept of what the church is trying to accomplish, because no one communicates it to them.

Involving the members has become more difficult. The nominating committee has become the most frustrating committee of the church. No one wants to serve on it because they know how difficult it is to get people to accept positions within the church. The older members feel they have done their part, and the younger ones are too busy to get that involved. If anyone comes up with a new idea, they are immediately told, "We have tried that before, and it doesn't work," or "We don't do it that way around here." Thus most new ideas are crushed before they can start.

Few new programs are initiated, and the existing ones have ceased to be effective anymore. Yet some of the members still feel hopeful for their church. They are unwilling to concede that the church has entered old age. However, this stage becomes very obvious when the church actually begins to experience a decline in attendance.

The final stage, death, is the most difficult for a church. No church wants to think that it will cease to exist. Yet all churches eventually will die. One of the few Seventh-day Adventist churches that have survived from the earliest days is the Washington, New Hampshire, church, the first Adventist church. It is still an actual church, but continues to exist solely because it is a museum. It would have died a long time ago if it were not preserved as our first church; it has ceased to be a vibrant church of the Advent hope.

Churches in the final two stages of life are caught up in institutionalization. The members look back on the glory days of the church, and as they look back they discover what the church did that made it so vibrant. Then they institutionalize it and declare that if the church today would just do what it did in the past, it would be vibrant again. However, what they fail to notice is that the things the church did in the beginning were in response to the needs of that era. Those needs changed, but the church did not. To be in harmony with its activities of the past, the church needs to reinvent itself to meet the needs of the present world. Yet most churches are unable to do this; therefore, they die.

Remembering the past is also an interesting phenomenon, for we have selective memories. We tend to remember either only the good or only the bad. Many times the past was not as good as people remember it. I recall that at one church where I pastored I was told how bad the previous pastor had been. I, the present pastor, was the only one worse. However, I quickly discovered that as one went back in their history, the earlier pastors were remembered as being much better than the later ones. In fact, I returned to this church 20 years later and discovered that I too had finally arrived at sainthood. Nostalgia is very much a part of these final two stages of the life cycle. You will notice that I have deliberately overlapped these stages. The reason is that movement from one to another is continuous. The final stage is only an intensification of the fourth stage.

Where Is Your Church?

After reading through these descriptions of the different stages of a life cycle, ask yourself which one best describes your church. You will find that the answer won't be completely clear-cut. You will find remnants of stage 2 when you are in stage 3, and so on, but it should be clear which one of them best describes your church.

If your church is in stage 1 or 2, it is still in a very healthy condition and probably does not need to seek renewal at this point. You can rejoice, but at the same time be on the alert for any indication that the church might be starting to move toward stage 3. Try to keep your church in stage 2 as long as possible.

If your church is in stage 3, remember that you still have many fruitful years ahead, but the process of death has already begun to creep into your congregation. The good news is that churches in stage 3 are much easier to turn around than those in stages 4 or 5. Mission is still fairly strong in the background of your church, so you must immediately begin to refocus on accomplishing your mission before the church moves further down the death track.

Stage 3 is very comfortable. It is hard to imagine that the seeds of death have been sown. The cycle is moving forward so insidiously that the church doesn't even realize it is happening. However, your church is not alone as it rides this plateau. Fully 80 to 85 percent of all Adventist churches in North America are plateaued or declining. This is why church renewal is such a significant issue for the Seventh-day Adventist Church. Unless we plant a multitude of new churches or renew our existing churches, the Adventist Church in the developed world will enter a period of decline and death. This must not be allowed to happen.

If your church is in stage 4 or 5, it is in serious trouble, even if you still have several hundred attending. Some churches move downward more quickly than others, but in general the road to vibrancy and health is going to be much more difficult than for a church still riding the plateau. In fact, if the church has declined too far it may even be beyond hope of redemption. It will die, and the best thing you can do is celebrate what it has accomplished and close the doors.

Fortunately, a church usually has one final chance at renewal before it enters the death spiral. If that opportunity passes, it is usually too late. I remember one such church. When they asked me to help, they were in the final stages of decline. This church was about to have its last chance.

The church had a beautiful sanctuary that seated 500 people. The members remembered the glory days when one had to come early for a seat, but now the 50 people attending weekly were lost in the large sanctuary, even with the back half of the church roped off. At our first meeting, the members told me that I was their last hope and that if my ideas did not work, they would have to close their doors. At least they recognized their desperate situation.

After I worked with the congregation for a couple years, they began to experience some growth. Their attendance began to climb, and approached the 150 mark. They now felt comfortable again—the bills were being paid and repairs could be made on the church—so they relaxed. They no longer needed my help. They had arrived, again. However, this church had really moved back only to stage 3, not to the growth of stage 2. They quickly slipped back down when they ceased to be a mission agency, and became a maintenance organization again.

There can be no retreat from mission. The minute a church moves away from accomplishing the mission of Christ it loses its way and heads quickly down the track toward death. When Jesus established His church as a mission agency, there could be no turning back. We cannot move from mission to maintenance; we must move from maintenance to mission if we are to continue to be a vibrant movement of God.

So what does a church do when it finds itself over the hill in the life cycle? How can we begin to move the church back toward the accomplishment of its mission? How can the church once again become an exciting congregation infused with Holy Spirit power? Someone suggests that we need to pray—and we must. Renewal must be bathed continually in prayer or it will not happen, but we must go a step further. There must also be visible action. The church must cooperate with the Holy Spirit in making the needed changes so the church can be renewed. If the church is unwilling to make changes, it cannot be renewed.

In the next chapter we will examine what can be done

if a church finds itself in stages 3, 4, or 5 in the life cycle. The ideal is to move back to stage 2, the stage of growth. How is that possible? How can renewal occur in plateaued and declining congregations? Our journey will continue as the next chapter examines the road to vitality.

[1] Roger Dudley, "How Churches Grow," *Ministry,* July 1981, p. 6.

[2] Phillip Barron Jones, "An Examination of the Statistical Growth of the Southern Baptist Convention," in *Understanding Church Growth and Decline,* ed. Dean Hoge and David Roozen (New York: Pilgrim Press, 1979), p. 170.

[3] *Ibid.,* p. 171.

4

Coming Out of Midlife Crisis

So you have determined that your church is in midlife crisis or, even worse, decline. What do you do? Is there any hope? Rest assured, there is a way out. It may not be easy, but by the grace of God you can move your church back to faithfulness and vibrancy. It will take a lot of work, so don't think it will be easy, but many things worth doing are not easy. And re-creating a mission-driven church is certainly worth doing.

Actually, you have already taken the first step to renewal. You have moved past the denial stage by actually reading this book up to this point. As you pondered the stages of the life cycle in the previous chapter, you clearly saw your church in stage 3, 4, or 5. The first step in renewal is the recognition that you have a problem. Most churches exist in total denial. In their eyes everything seems to be going fine. The church is filled. The bank accounts are adequate. Why all the fuss? You have crossed that barrier by recognizing that your church does have a problem.

What if you recognize the problem but the rest of the church does not? You cannot go it alone. Lone rangers rarely accomplish the turnaround of a church. You are going to need an initiating group that realizes that something must be done. The next step is to get others on board with you. Look over your membership. Who else do you sense has a real burden for the church to fulfill its mission? Talk to that person. Share this book or give them a copy. Get them on board.

Which people you get to join you in the quest for renewal is very important. You cannot select just anyone. You need the right people. Who are these individuals? They are your key leaders, and it depends on the size of your church as to who fits the definition of a key leader. In a larger church you must obviously make certain the pastor is with you, while in a smaller church you must include the key leader whom everyone follows. The full cooperation of your major leadership is required to bring about the kind of change needed to facilitate the church's return to its mission roots.

As your initiating group begins to meet and study through the material in this book, they will start to grasp a clearer picture of where the church is now and where it should go if it is to return to being a mission-centered church. Once you are in agreement that your church is in stage 3, 4, or 5, and you reach a decision that you want to return to stage 2, you are ready to move on to the next steps to vibrancy.

Possible Intervention Events

Having determined there is a problem, you need to consider the best time to initiate the transformation into a mission-centered church. There are several events that provide the best possibility for starting the renewal process.[1] An intervention event will not immediately turn the church around, but it usually offers a special window of opportunity that will make it easier to move the church forward than at other times. What are some of these opportune times?

An obvious point for transformation is the arrival of a new pastor. People expect change to occur when the new pastor arrives, so this may be a good time to initiate the move. You will need to make certain the new pastor is in agreement with the change, or, if you are the new pastor, you will need to make certain your key leaders are in agreement, but this time of transition provides a golden opportunity that should not be passed by. The new pastor, who has nothing to defend from the past, has a clean slate and can without bias help the church recognize areas that need change. In fact, Barna discovered that in all the churches that were declining, the turnaround occurred with the arrival of a new pastor.[2]

Another moment of receptivity is during a church revival. At this time the Holy Spirit manifests Himself in special power to a church. The presence of the Spirit always leads the church back to its mission. Remember that Jesus has sent the Holy Spirit to enable the church to accomplish Christ's mission. Interestingly, every genuine revival in history has resulted in people coming to Jesus. Genuine revival always results in soul winning; false revivals can create warm feelings, but they do not lead to the advancement of the kingdom of God.

Of course, genuine revivals cannot be manufactured; they must be "prayed down." Thus your initiating group should spend much time praying for your church and for a revival of Holy Spirit power. An even better situation is to have a revival occur with the advent of a new pastor. Two possible intervention events occurring at the same time obviously will make it easier to turn the church in a new direction. Remember, the Spirit always initiates new beginnings.

A crisis in the church can also lead to a new orientation. It does not matter what kind of crisis—church burning down, a moral problem in the leadership, a financial scandal, etc. Shared problems help a church move toward renewal. However, do not manufacture a crisis to accomplish this. You will regret burning down the church! Nevertheless, if you find your church in crisis, this may be the time to think of initiating the new movement to a mission orientation.

The sharing of this renewal information with the church is another time that new beginnings can occur. Take the time to plot out the growth history of the church over a 10-year span. Members will be surprised to see a flat line or a leveling off of the growth curve. They may not have realized what has been happening. This can lead them to want to take the church in a new direction. You may also wish to share how much of the church's budget is going into mission and how much into maintenance. Sharing this information with the church board or even the wider membership can spark new beginnings. However, never attempt to share the information with the whole church unless and until you have first shared it with the leadership and they are in agreement with the idea of presenting it to the rest of the church. You will never turn a church around by bypassing the current leadership.

Renewal can also happen when a church decides to plant a church. When this happens, the church will be losing some members and finances. That reality can disrupt stagnation. It means that the church needs to attract some new members immediately, or the attendance and finances will be down. These circumstances can help to shift the church back into mission mode. However, be careful here. As soon as the church regains what it lost with the new church plant, it could easily drift back to maintenance. In this instance, don't just try a quick fix to get some new members; use the event to initiate systemic change in the church that will push it back into a mission mentality once again.

These intervention events will not turn the church around. They are simply good times to initiate the change back to a mission orientation. If two or more of these events take place at the same time, it will always be easier to move the church forward, so watch for these golden opportunities. Some of these happenings must be taken advantage of when they occur, and some you can initiate. If you are successful in moving the church back to stage 2, you have created a new life cycle for your church. But you will have to be on the alert constantly, for Satan will attempt to move you back to maintenance.

Remember, turning the church around will take less time if your church is on a plateau than if it is in decline mode. The further down the decline ladder your church has gone, the more difficult it will be to bring it back up. However, three years should be sufficient to turn it around.[3] If it can't be done in three years, then it probably is one of the churches that can't be turned around. It may continue on a plateau for several years, but then slip into total decline. The exception would be an institutional church. It can appear to have vibrancy because of its association with an institution. This can camouflage the real problem. It will appear to be healthy and vibrant, but underneath it can be dead.

Why is it more difficult to turn around a church that is in decline than one that is on a plateau? When a church moves into decline, most members have begun to realize that they are in trouble. The recognition begins with a touch of nostalgia as people begin to remember what the church was like when Pastor Alex was there. When you hear these words of nostalgia, it means that people are beginning to recognize that the church is not what it used to be.

As the decline intensifies, people begin to suggest that if certain things were done, the church would quickly be back to where it was before. The problem is that each person mentions something different. So differing views on the reason for the decline begin to develop. Some of them may be right; others may not. This is not the problem. There has been no real study as to why the church is slipping, just different people suggesting different reasons.

As the decline becomes serious, the church begins to polarize into warring camps. Each camp rallies around a different rationale for the decline. Rather than do anything about any of the issues involved, the church members spar off with each other, casting blame on anything other than themselves. When a church reaches this stage of decline, it is on the verge of collapse, and it becomes nearly impossible to turn it around. This is why we advocate initiating the move to renewal before the situation deteriorates to this level. After the warring camps wear out, the church usually closes its doors. It is the end.

Hopefully, your church is not that far down the ladder of decline. The advantage of the decline position is that the church realizes it has a problem; however, the members are fighting so badly that they don't want to do anything productive. On the other hand, the plateaued church is easier to turn around, yet it is in denial of its problems. Neither situation is going to be easy.

Remember, however, that we operate not in human strength but in divine power. This is not your church; it is Jesus' church. He is the head of the church, and He will bring us through the difficult times to renew our commitment to His mission. After we have recognized the need to renew the church, the most important step forward is to re-create the dream. That is the focus of our next chapter.

---

[1] Aubrey Malphurs, *Pouring New Wine Into Old Wineskins* (Grand Rapids: Baker Books, 1993), pp. 113-125.

[2] G. Barna, *Turn-Around Churches,* p. 47.

[3] *Ibid.,* p. 41.

5

Re-creating the Dream

Whenever a church is on the downside of its life cycle, the only remedy to renewal is to go back and re-create a dream for the church. Most churches began with a dream to accomplish something for God, but over the years the dream was forgotten in the daily routine of running the church. If your church is in stage 3, 4, or 5 in its life cycle, and you have made the decision to attempt to move back to stage 2—the growth stage—then the process must always work through the creation of the dream.

When a church has plateaued, it may be able simply to rekindle the dream that it had in the beginning. But if the plateau has continued for several years or if the church is in decline, it is not sufficient simply to revive the old dream. The church must go back to the beginning and start from scratch with a new dream or vision.* If few people can even remember what the dream was, then you should definitely start over with a new dream. In fact, if you are in doubt at all, start with a fresh dream.

Four Questions

In order to help a church re-create the dream, there are four questions that need to be asked. It would be helpful for the church leadership to work their way through each of these questions.

Question 1: *Why are we here?* Spend time discussing why your church exists. You may feel that everyone knows the reason, but as you ask the question and people begin to share, you will quickly discover that there are various understandings among the members as to the reason for your existence. Many churches are not accomplishing anything of value because they have never worked through this question to arrive at a consensus as to why they exist.

You cannot assume anything here—you need to work your way through the discussion of this question. After members have shared some of their views on why the church is here, it is helpful to ask them to support their understanding with Scripture.

You see, it is not enough just to have everyone agree on why the church exists, especially if we have only shared our opinion. Adventism is a biblical movement, and as such we must base our understanding of the church's existence on Scripture. Remember, this is not really your church; it is the Lord's church. We are His followers. His purpose for the church must be our purpose. To have any other purpose for the church than His is to fail to be a legitimate church of Jesus Christ.

Hopefully, your discussion will lead you to the Great Commission, in which Jesus, with great force, outlines the purpose of the church—to make disciples. Any other purpose than that which the Founder of Christianity gives is a misdirected purpose. If you will allow the church leadership to discuss this issue long enough, most of them will eventually come to Matthew 28:16-20. Instinctively we know in the deepest recesses of our minds that the church exists to fulfill the Great Commission, but many have forgotten. This is why question 1 is so crucial.

The second question follows: *Where will our present course take us?* In other words, if we keep doing what we are doing, what will we look like in five years? In asking this question of churches that are plateaued or declining, I have always received similar answers. The plateaued churches will respond that they will probably be at about the same place, and the declining churches usually say they will not be here at all. These are important conclusions, because they clearly indicate that something needs to change.

As the discussion of this question proceeds, the chairperson needs to make certain that the group is focusing on where the present course will lead in conjunction with the reason for the existence of the church that was established through discussion of the first question. If a plateaued or declining church cannot look down the road and see itself making disciples with increased intensity, it will be disobedient to Jesus' great commission, an unacceptable position for a church that claims to follow the Master.

The third question usually can be answered very quickly: *Is this where we want to go?* Do we really want to be in the same condition five years from now? Adventists are called by God to prepare a people for the Second Coming. If we live within this belief, then our churches can never be satisfied with the status quo, and it will be absolutely untenable for them to be in decline.

The fourth and final question is then very critical. Having determined the reason for our existence and that our present course is not in harmony with our purpose, we realize we don't want to go down that road. Therefore, *in order to fulfill our destiny as a church, what must be changed?* Please note that change is not to be sought for the sake of change, but change must bring about the fulfillment of our mission. This mission consciousness is what must drive the change process.

Visioning for the Future

The path to re-creating a vision that we have just suggested is important because it helps the church focus in the right direction. Many churches have begun the visioning process with no reference to Jesus' purpose for the church. The result is that they end up with a nice-sounding vision statement, but one that could send the church down the wrong road instead of leading toward the fulfillment of the Great Commission.

In entering the visioning process with a church, purpose must always be paramount. This vision is for the accomplishment of the mission of Christ. The process must begin by looking at what the church would be like if it embraced God's vision. A helpful exercise at this stage is to have the leaders write a short paragraph describing the church as they see it in five years, if it lived up to God's ideal for it.

After each leader has written their paragraph, have each one read it to the rest of the group. The group should be looking for areas of commonality. No one should ridicule any suggestion made by another person or demean anyone's vision. The point here is to share each individual vision for the church in accordance with God's purpose for the church. You will be surprised to discover the level of harmony that will be seen in these statements. It is from these areas of agreement that you should begin to build your vision for the church collectively. It is not a matter of simply adopting one person's vision—it is vitally important that all the leadership have input in the development of the vision.

Once the shared vision has been created, then some hard work needs to begin. The question must be posed: How do we arrive at our goal in five years? Start with the vision and work backwards—where should you be in four years, three years, two years, and one year? As each level is put in place, you should also list what needs to be done in order to attain the goal for each year. Each action step needs to be assigned a date for completion and an individual appointed who is responsible to see that it happens.

Sharing the Vision With the Church

Once the church leadership has developed the vision and a plan for reaching that goal, the hard work is done. Now the new vision needs to find wider acceptance in the whole church. I have found that if the leadership is totally committed to the idea, the people will follow. During this stage many sermons on the mission of the church should be preached, helping the church regain a sense of mission direction. After the mission mind-set has been instilled, it is then possible to begin to introduce the vision that the leadership has so carefully developed.

Please remember that this process is not just a matter of putting together a nice vision statement that can be framed and hung up on the wall of the church. The vision statement is a working document. It is not just a pleasant-sounding paragraph; it is a vision of where we want our church to be in the next five years and a plan to get there. Congregations always respond to vision.

Your new vision may necessitate new programs, new plans, new finances, etc. Let these things develop out of the need to fulfill the vision. Don't protect anything the church already had in place. Anything that is not in harmony with or helping the church accomplish the new vision will need to be discarded. Just as the programs, finances, etc., arose from the mission need when the church began, so it must happen now.

Creating Change

Many books have been written on creating change in a church. I do not intend to replicate them here. I refer the reader to any excellent resource on change that will be helpful. However, I wish to mention a few things you should remember as you attempt to move the church off the plateau and create the changes needed to accomplish that feat.

The process I have described in this chapter is an excellent way to bring about change in a church. However, there are a few added cautions. Change is created differently, depending on the size of the church. Exceptions are always possible, but these are good general rules. In small churches of less than 50 people attending, a matriarch or a patriarch usually rules the church. They have considerable influence, and no change will happen in their church without their involvement and approval. These are the ones who speak, and as soon as they give their opinion the rest of the leadership lines up behind them. Unless they are on board, the church will not move forward. Many of these people are wonderful individuals who have the best intentions and want the church to grow. If the matriarch in the church is positive about helping the church move back to growth, she will be a great asset in realizing the goal. On the other hand, if the patriarch is negative toward change, few churches will be able to override his influence.

In churches with 50-400 in attendance, the collective church leadership usually makes decisions. This type of congregation is too large for any one person to dominate, so differences are ironed out by the church board. The method for change that I have outlined in this chapter is the primary one to use with a church of this size. I focused on this model because most Adventist churches are within this size range.

Churches with more than 400 in attendance are too big to iron out details in the church board. Such churches usually follow the guidance of the initiating leader, who is generally the senior pastor. This is not to say that the pastor works alone. The pastor must take the leadership with him or her, but the members will usually follow if they trust him or her. This methodology works only for the large church, so small-church pastors should not try it or they will encounter serious problems.

In summary, if your church is a small church, work through the matriarch or patriarch to accomplish the change. If your church is a midsize church, change will occur by working through the major leaders of the church. If your church is a large church, then the pastor becomes the initiating leader to bring about the change.

How to Lead a Church Forward

Taking leaders with you as you lead a church to vitality is essential, but just how do you accomplish it? The suggestions already offered are vital, but there are some added points that will aid you as you attempt to get your leadership on board with the move to vitality.

Churches must not be led like secular organizations. Churches are spiritual entities, and they must be led spiritually. You can learn from secular leaders, but the process you follow must include spiritual development. As you are attempting to move your church into mission, there must at the same time be a movement to increase the spirituality of the membership. Revival and spiritual momentum under the power of the Holy Spirit are essential ingredients in the renewal process. You cannot manufacture a revival, but you can certainly get people praying for one. Revival does not just happen; revival occurs in response to the powerful prayers of God's people. So find the members with the spiritual gift of intercession and get them praying for a revival in your church.

Don't keep silent. Let the entire congregation know that many are praying for this revival of the Spirit. Others will begin to join in the prayer for revival. Prayer movements always precede powerful revivals. As more people begin to pray for revival and Holy Spirit power, a new force will begin to be seen in the church; and bear in mind, the power of the Holy Spirit always leads the church back into mission. So remember, in the process of leading the church forward, be certain to provide the spiritual momentum to accompany all that you do to bring the church to renewal.

Another important factor in moving forward is to research the history of the church. Discover what they were doing in the past that was successful. The instruction of Jesus to the church at Ephesus was to do the first work. Again we are not talking about cloning what the church did 30 years ago, but out of the ashes of that mighty time when God worked in the church, you can find something to build on that will enable you to create a vision for the future. Churches that are successful in the renewal process affirm the past as they move forward.

Sometimes new leaders assume that everything the church has done in the past has been bad, but this is not true. Without a doubt, the church is involved in many good things. We need to affirm the past while simultaneously changing those things that are no longer beneficial. For example, many churches have learned that it is difficult to say goodbye to an old building, even though everyone knows that it needs to be replaced. The building has become a sacred place to the members. They were baptized there, they were married there, dad's funeral was held there—and the reminiscing continues. To tear down the church is to lose those memories.

What should be done? Wise churches incorporate

some of the old into the new building. They might make the new pulpit out of the old pews or create a heritage room where a stained-glass window from the old church is placed. This helps people move into the future while still honoring the past. This is extremely important in any move toward vitality.

Now focus on the five-year plan you have put together. You will be moving steadily toward the accomplishment of that vision, but five years is a long time. It is easy to become waylaid along the road. There must, therefore, be times of celebration as parts of the vision are accomplished. This will allow the congregation to rejoice that progress has been made toward the ultimate goal. In the early stages I would suggest having celebrations every six months. This would be a time when the congregation is informed of the progress they have made. As the church celebrates step by step the five years will pass, and the church will finally find its vision fulfilled.

It is interesting to note that churches frequently conduct celebrations like this for the accomplishment of monetary goals but rarely for mission goals. Many churches will have a big thermometer up front, and every week or every month the red line is raised, showing how the church is progressing toward the ultimate goal of the project. This is a good thing and very important. We all understand that it is necessary in order to raise the needed funds. What we are suggesting here is that similar methodology be developed that will allow churches to keep their congregation up-to-date on any progress made toward establishing the new vision.

By now you are probably thinking that this process of renewal is a lot of work. It is. From the beginning we have heard that it will not be easy and will involve a lot of hard work. However, the rewards are out of this world! Imagine the new vitality that will be coming to

your church! Imagine the thrill of seeing your church actively involved in the fulfillment of the mission of Christ!
Imagine the new people coming to Jesus and ultimately
becoming a part of the kingdom of God! Is it worth it?
Every bone in my body cries out: Let it happen now!
Don't live another moment in idleness when the power
of the Holy Spirit stands ready to help you move forward
to the accomplishment of the new vision that God is
about to create for your church.

---

* A. Malphurs, *Pouring New Wine Into Old Wineskins,* p. 133.

6
Where Do We Go From Here?

So now your church has a dream. A dream is one thing. Reality is something else. Before you proceed any further you should do a reality check. Is your dream focused in the right direction? Will it help you facilitate the accomplishment of Christ's mission? What are the hindrances that will keep you from accomplishing the vision God has given your church? These issues must be addressed before you proceed any further in the accomplishment of the vision.

Some churches instinctively know their weaknesses, but others need help in determining their weak spots. A useful tool that allows the church to discover problem areas on the road back to vibrancy is the book *Natural Church Development*.[1] The whole focus of natural church development (NCD) is on creating healthy churches.[2] NCD enables the church to discover its weaknesses scientifically by utilizing a survey instrument. This instrument is based on an extensive research project that has been designed to discover what makes churches healthy. The study revealed that there are eight quality characteristics that are present in healthy, growing churches. The NCD survey instrument evaluates how well the church is doing in each of the quality characteristics, in comparison with other churches.

The premise of the NCD research is that a church should begin working on its weakest area, realizing that the weakest link is hindering the church from growth. In fact, Adventist churches that have utilized the principles learned through NCD have significantly improved their health as a result of working on their minimum factor (in the NCD study the weakest area is termed the *minimum factor*). As you begin to move your church toward the accomplishment of its vision, it is very important to discover which areas should be addressed first as you strive to improve the health of the church.

Some might be wondering if their church should take the NCD survey before creating the dream.[3] This approach could work in some churches, but I personally believe it would be better to create the dream first. Once the members have a mission mind-set they are apt to take the results of the NCD survey much more seriously. If a church takes the survey before creating the dream, the result could be an attitude of indifference when the results are learned. It is amazing how attitudes in the church change once a mission mind-set is restored to the church. This is why it is imperative for the church to go through the visioning process first and then begin to identify and address their weakest areas.

NCD has identified eight quality characteristics of growing churches. In my book on NCD I have expounded adequately on each of the characteristics. I will not repeat that information here, but instead just give you a quick summary of each of the quality characteristics. The first is *empowering leadership.* It is a leadership that seeks to empower other people for ministry rather than attempt to do it all by oneself. The second characteristic is closely related: *gift-oriented ministry.* It is helping people discover their spiritual gift and then utilize that gift in a relevant area of ministry.

The third characteristic is *passionate spirituality*. It is a vibrant faith that is developed when people have been touched by God and love to fellowship with Him in Bible study and prayer, both collectively and individually. The fourth characteristic is that of *functional structures*. This characteristic examines the structural formation of the church to make certain its organization, including boards and committees, is supportive of the mission of the church.

The fifth characteristic is *inspiring worship*. This type of worship results when church members have been placed in touch with the infinite God of the universe. These people love to come to church. Worship is an exciting, happy time for them. The sixth characteristic is holistic *small groups*. "Small groups" primarily refers to the church creating a safe place where people can be themselves, relating openly and honestly with one another without fear of criticism or rejection.

The last two characteristics are *need-oriented evangelism* and *loving relationships*. Need-oriented evangelism involves the church having a mission mind-set and focusing its evangelism on the needs of lost people. Loving relationships obviously refers to the interpersonal relationships that exist in the church, for Christ's church must always be a place of love and care.

Taking the NCD survey will reveal where your church scores in each one of these characteristics. Once that is known, the church can begin working on the minimum factor. As it works on that characteristic, the church will see a reverberating effect on all the other characteristics, and the church's health will improve in each area. If the church is low in any characteristic, it will be unable to accomplish its vision or dream fully until that area has improved, so dealing with the minimum factor is of vital importance in helping a church move off the plateau and into mission accomplishment.

The scoring of the NCD survey is built on a median of 50. If a church scores above 50 in one characteristic, it is above average in that area; below 50 would be below average as compared with other churches. Few churches ever score significantly over 50. In fact, in compiling the data from hundreds of North American Division Adventist churches, we have discovered that Adventist churches generally score slightly below the 50 mark. Fortunately, we have seen a few churches score significantly above 50, but obviously these are unusual churches. Most churches score between 35 and 65, so a church scoring in that grid would be considered average.

Which characteristics do Adventists churches do better in than others? And likewise, which are generally our worst characteristics? After scoring the surveys for hundreds of Adventist churches, the North American Division Evangelism Institute (NADEI) has developed some helpful statistics. The following table shows the av-

CHARACTERISTIC	AVERAGE
Need-oriented Evangelism	48
Passionate Spirituality	46
Empowering Leadership	42
Loving Relationships	41
Inspiring Worship	37
Functional Structures	37
Gift-oriented Ministry	35
Holistic Small Groups	33

erage for Adventist churches in each characteristic:

From the table above it appears that Adventist churches generally are stronger in the areas of need-oriented evangelism and passionate spirituality. This is a good thing. However, even our best scores are slightly below the median. Our worst areas are gift-oriented ministry and holistic small groups. It would seem that these two areas are in need of special attention in most Adventist churches.

Remember that these scores are averages for all the Adventist churches that have taken the NCD survey. Individual churches have scored well above these averages, while others have scored significantly below the averages. So that you can grasp the wide variation, the chart below reveals the highest and lowest scores we have recorded for Adventist churches in each of the

CHARACTERISTIC	HIGHEST SCORE	LOWEST SCORE
Empowering Leadership	78	–18
Gift-oriented Ministry	76	–12
Passionate Spirituality	86	11
Functional Structures	75	6
Inspiring Worship	74	2
Holistic Small Groups	84	–14
Need-oriented Evangelism	86	12
Loving Relationships	88	4

eight quality characteristics.

Amazingly, the highest score ever recorded on any characteristic was for loving relationships with a high score of 88, while the lowest ever recorded was in empowering leadership with a score of -18. The contrast between these scores reveals some very healthy Adventist churches and some in desperate need of revival. One may wonder how a church could end up with a minus score. That is because the scoring is based on a median of 50 and not a percentage. Thus the -18 represents a church that is 68 points below median.

Does it make a difference when a church works on its minimum factor? The following chart contrasts the averages between the two scores in churches that have worked on their minimum factor and then repeated the survey.

Chart 1
SEVENTH-DAY ADVENTISTS IN THE U.S.A.
NCD Average Scores (Only 1 and 2 Tests)

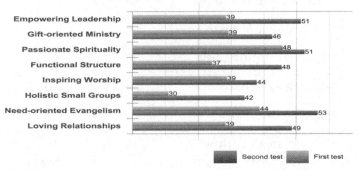

NADEI (2003)

A quick examination of chart 1 reveals that when churches work seriously on their minimum factor they experience significant change in their health status. These averages represent dramatic shifts from churches that are serious about improving church health. They reveal that changing the health of a church is not a pipe dream, but can be an actual reality. However, there have been a few churches that have not worked on their weaknesses but merely retaken the survey a year later. Interestingly, their second survey results are very close to the first results, which indicates that a church must work seriously on the minimum factor if it is to experience significant growth.

An examination of the Adventist NCD data results in some interesting conclusions. One surprising result is that the larger in attendance a church is, the healthier it appears to be. For some reason small Adventist churches suffer more ill health than larger churches. Notice the following chart. The quality of every characteristic improves with an increase in attendance. Larger churches generally are healthier churches. This does not mean that small churches can't be healthy, but it appears that in the Adventist setting, larger churches generally have better church health.

Chart 2
SEVENTH-DAY ADVENTISTS IN THE U.S.A.—
Comparison
Number of Church Attendants

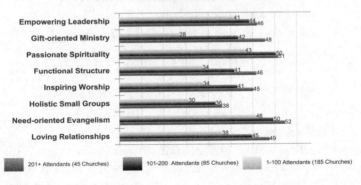

NADEI (2003)

The attitude of a church also impacts its health. Healthy churches, for example, have a much more positive attitude toward change. In fact, resistance to change is a major barrier to good health. It seems that churches open to change are healthier because they are willing to implement the changes needed to accomplish better health, whereas churches resistant to change have a tendency to avoid making the changes that would bring about better health. The following chart reveals how a church reacts to change and how it affects its health in each of the characteristics. Notice that the more optimistic a church is about change, the higher it scores in each of the characteristics.

Chart 3
SEVENTH-DAY ADVENTISTS IN THE U.S.A.— Comparison
Churches' View of Change

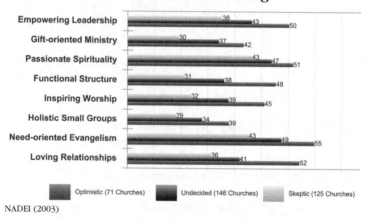

NADEI (2003)

It also appears that each year the churches taking the survey are scoring higher than in previous years. This may be because churches that were aware of their problems had the tendency to take the survey when it first became available through NADEI, whereas today a more representative number of churches are completing the survey. The following chart records the score in each characteristic for those who took the survey in each of the years listed. The numbers for 2003 are for the first half of the year only.

Quantities	Average Scores					
(Only First Tests)	1998-1999	2000	2001	2002	2003	Total
Empowering Leadership	33	41	42	43	45	42
Gift-oriented Ministry	33	32	29	35	42	34
Passionate Spirituality	44	45	43	46	52	46
Functional Structure	32	38	35	37	40	36
Inspiring Worship	34	37	36	37	40	37
Holistic Small Groups	27	33	30	34	35	33
Need-oriented Evangelism	41	48	46	48	51	47
Loving Relationships	35	42	42	41	43	41
Number of Churches	37	44	61	124	54	320

Three areas of concern are the characteristics for holistic small groups, gift-oriented ministry, and inspiring worship services. As we examine the Adventist data collected thus far, it appears that these characteristics are among Adventism's lowest characteristics. Yet it appears that if churches are healthy in these areas, they are also healthy in most other areas. In other words, the data suggests that working on these particular characteristics will have a reverberating effect on all the others.

To examine this data further, we pulled out those churches that had high scores in inspiring worship services, gift-oriented ministry, and holistic small groups. We then averaged all their characteristics in each of the eight qualities. We discovered that they were also high in all the additional quality characteristics. Notice the three charts with the results of the averages for these three characteristics.

Chart 4
SEVENTH-DAY ADVENTISTS IN THE U.S.A—
Comparison
Seeker-sensitive Worship Service

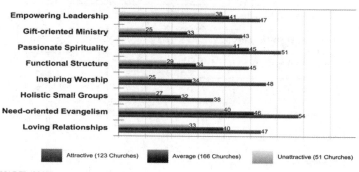

NADEI (2003)

Chart 5
SEVENTH-DAY ADVENTISTS IN THE U.S.A.—
Comparison
Participation in Small Groups

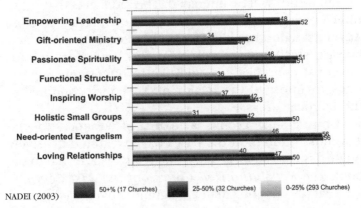

NADEI (2003)

Chart 6
SEVENTH-DAY ADVENTISTS IN THE U.S.A.—
Comparison
Utilization of Spiritual Gifts

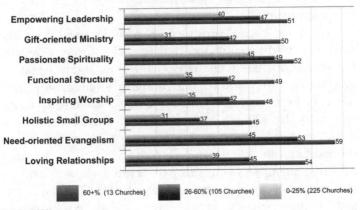

NADEI (2003)

When these characteristics are high, there is a corresponding lift to all the other characteristics. This means that if a church can concentrate on improving the worship service, gift-based ministry, and small groups, its overall health will be upgraded. The sad fact is that these three characteristics are generally below average in most Adventist churches. In fact, gift-oriented ministry and holistic small groups represent the lowest scores for Adventist churches. I would like to offer some suggestions to improve the health of Adventist churches in these crucial areas.

Holistic small groups is an area of weakness for the Adventist Church. In the past I have written extensively on the issue of small groups. The reader is referred to my book *The Revolutionized Church of the 21st Century*[4] for that discussion. Many longtime Adventists see no need for involvement in a small group because they already have many relationships within the church. However, this is not true for the newcomer. The result is that the older members do not make small groups available for the newcomers because they see no need for them, and thus many new people fail to make inroads into the church.

Yet holistic small groups were a vital part of the early Adventist church and one that was absolutely essential for their spiritual well-being. Churches today need to give serious attention to incorporating small groups into the very fabric of their church if they are serious about restoring the church to health. It is not necessary for these small groups to be home groups, although that is the easiest way to accomplish improvement in the area of small groups. Even Sabbath school classes can be holistic small groups, although most do not fit this category. Holistic small groups create a safe place where people can be themselves and grow in Christ without condemnation. This can happen in a Sabbath school class, but most Adventist classes deal only with information and therefore are not holistic.

The other aspect of small groups that needs attention in Adventist circles is that of multiplying the small groups. Some Adventist churches incorporate small groups into their church program, but fail to multiply the groups. This is an area in need of serious attention in most Adventist churches. Healthy groups multiply, whereas unhealthy groups turn inward. It is not enough to have small groups actively operating in your church; these groups must also be multiplying.

There is no stronger correlation to church growth than the multiplying of the group structure in the church. It is impossible to grow a healthy, vibrant Adventist church today without small groups as a vital part of its ministry. For further understanding in the area of small groups, the reader is referred to my book mentioned above or any of the multitude of excellent books and resources on small groups available from the NADEI Resource Center at www.nadei.org.

The other area in which the Adventist Church scores the lowest on the NCD scale is gift-oriented ministry. The next two chapters will examine this very important part of the formula for church growth.

[1] Christian Schwartz, *Natural Church Development* (St. Charles, Ill.: Church Smart Resources, 1996).

[2] Please consult my booklet on NCD, *Creating Healthy Adventist Churches Through Natural Church Development* (Berrien Springs, Mich.: North American Division Evangelism Institute, 2003). It is available from North American Evangelism Institute (NADEI), Andrews University, Berrien Springs, Michigan 49104.

[3] The Adventist version of the NCD survey is available from NADEI.

[4] Fallbrook, Calif.: Hart Research Center, 1997.

7

Gift-based Ministry and Renewal

Many churches have seen the need for a gift-based ministry and have realized that the laity must be empowered for ministry, but they have not known how to accomplish it."* In previous books and seminars I have spoken extensively about spiritual gifts and getting every member in ministry in harmony with their spiritual gifts. However, I have come to some additional conclusions regarding gift-based ministry that I would like to share in this volume, especially since the NCD scores for the characteristic of gift-oriented ministry are almost the lowest in Adventist churches. The problem for Adventists appears to be not in the area of identifying our gifts but in actually getting involved in ministry in harmony with one's giftedness. This is the area that I wish to address in this chapter.

The Scriptures reveal more than 20 spiritual gifts. Most attempts at gift-based ministry have concentrated on helping people discover which of the 20 or more gifts they possess. Whenever one takes a spiritual gifts inventory, it will usually reveal a cluster of gifts. Some of the gifts are even difficult to distinguish between, such as knowledge and wisdom.

Once the gifts are identified, then the question arises

as to how and where to use these gifts. For example, how does an individual use the gift of discernment in a ministry, or the gift of encouragement? Few of the gifts actually seem to attach themselves naturally to any particular ministry. Therefore, people need to decide which specific ministry best utilizes their gifts. This may be where the breakdown is occurring.

I would like to suggest that it is not as important to identify a particular gift as it is to discover what type of gift an individual possesses. My basic gift orientation is more important than a specific gift. I do not mean to say that there is no value in discovering a particular gift, but it is better to discover a person's basic gift orientation. Once that is clear, then an individual may wish to discover the actual gift(s) possessed.

What is meant by basic gift orientation? There are two basic gift orientations in Scripture: one who trains others, and one who does actual ministry. In previous books I have written extensively about the role of the pastor as a trainer. However, the training role is not limited to pastors. The Scriptures reveal that any member may have been gifted to train others. The basic training orientation is seen in the listing of the gifts mentioned in Ephesians 4:11, 12:

"And He gave some as apostles, and some as prophets, and some as evangelists, and some as pastors and teachers, for the equipping of the saints for the work of service, to the building up of the body of Christ."

In the other major New Testament passages that list the spiritual gifts (Romans 12 and 1 Corinthians 12), we see gifts of doing: teaching, ministry, helps, encouragement, discernment, etc. Yet in Ephesians 4 there is a remarkable difference—these are gifts not of doing but of training. The apostles, prophets, evangelists, and pastor-teachers listed here are people whom God has given to the church so that they can train the rest for ministry. In this case the gift is the person, not the activity they are doing.

This differentiation helps Adventists understand spiritual gifts a little better. For example, Adventists have had a difficult time with the gift of prophecy in spiritual gifts inventories. Many have made the unwarranted assumption that because one has the gift of prophecy, one is a prophet. However, there are really two separate gifts— the gift of prophet and the gift of prophecy. Most prophets also have the gift of prophecy, but most people who have the gift of prophecy do not have the gift of prophet. They are two separate gifts.

Likewise the gift of evangelist is one of the people gifts that God has given to accomplish the training of members for evangelism. Please note that in Scripture there is no gift of evangelism, only the gift of evangelist. Most inventories assume that these two are identical; they are not. All God's people are to be involved in evangelism; it is not the domain of a few who are gifted, but the responsibility of all who claim to be children of God. The gift of evangelist is not for the performance of evangelism, but instead to train the rest of us for the joy of winning people to Jesus, which is the responsibility of all Christians.

People whom God has gifted to be trainers are those described in Ephesians 4—the apostles, prophets, evangelists, pastors-teachers. These are not limited to clergy, for God has also gifted many members to train others. The rest of the gifts are the ministry gifts that enable people to engage in a special ministry for the Master. What are these gifts? All the rest that are mentioned in Scripture: wisdom, knowledge, faith, healing, miracles, discernment, tongues, interpretation, hospitality, administration, helps, prophecy, ministry, teaching, exhortation, giving, and mercy (see 1 Cor. 12:8-10, 28; 1 Peter 4:9, 10; and Rom. 12:6-8).

The main purpose of the gift discovery process should be to help people discover if they have a training gift or a ministry gift. Once that basic orientation is decided, then it is easier to discover what role the person should play in ministry, specifically, whether they should be engaged in training others or in performing a ministry. Knowing the exact ministry or exact spiritual gift is not as important as knowing one's basic orientation to ministry.

One of the biggest obstacles to the implementation of a gift-based ministry in the church has been the failure of people to realize their basic gift orientation. We have assumed that one with the gift of pastor or teacher should be pastoring or teaching. However, Ephesians 4 indicates that one who is a pastor should be training others to pastor rather than doing it all alone. Likewise, the one with the gift of teaching should be training other teachers who will actually teach, while the trainer continues to focus on training still other teachers.

Nothing is more frustrating than having an individual with the gift of training who is performing a ministry role or a person gifted to minister who is placed in a trainer role in the church. Probably the latter would be the more frustrating. For example, most churches choose as personal ministries leader a person who does a good job giving Bible studies and performing other evangelistic activities. No thought is given to whether or not the person would be a good trainer. The person is then placed in the leadership position.

It is expected that the personal ministries leader will involve many other members in personal evangelistic activities. But because the person in the position is a doer and not a trainer, the person ends up doing all the work. The individual gets frustrated and ends up leaving that ministry position. It would be better to choose someone who is not as good in personal evangelism but, instead, is good in mobilizing other people. When you make that person personal ministries leader, the ministry will hum. We could avoid much frustration if we would follow the plan of putting trainers in leadership roles and ministry people in ministry roles.

Yet it poses a problem to place people in the right roles. For example, many people serve in a role because that role provides the person with a power base. Certain ministry positions automatically place people on the church board. If I am not a trainer but I enjoy the power that comes from being on the church board, I might be reluctant to turn my position of power over to a trainer, because I would then lose my powerful standing in the church. No one likes to admit it, but this is one of the biggest problems the church faces in getting the right people into the right positions.

What can be done? The first thing I would suggest is to remove power from ministry positions. Do not tie seats on the church board to ministry positions. I realize that to do so would be contrary to the *Church Manual's* current recommendations. However, any church can ask their conference for permission to try something new. Most conferences are willing to help a church with new, innovative approaches. Today there is widespread frustration with the current system in the church, and many recognize that changes need to be made. However, we must do so in cooperation with the leadership of the church.

How can you remove power from ministry positions? Elect your church board separately from other church positions. This could also help you to reduce the size of your church board. Most churches have too many people on the church board. The result is that few people even show up for many board meetings. Elect those you want to hold accountable for how the church is run, but then appoint people to ministry teams with the appropriate people as trainer leaders and ministry performers. Of course, if the church were perfect, this would all happen naturally, but unfortunately the church is filled with sinners like me, and a less-than-perfect church exists; therefore, people end up serving in the wrong roles.

How can one tell if they possess a trainer gift or a ministry gift? Most people know that intuitively, and most of us who know each other in the church unconsciously know this about our fellow believers. It really does not take some elaborate instrument to tell if I possess training or ministry gifts. Trainers are always trying to get other people into ministry. They enjoy delegating tasks to others, valuing what others do—and their juices really flow when they see the people they have trained succeed. On the other hand, those with ministry gifts are always looking for someone to help them. They do not like to lead out, but they are happy to follow if someone would only show them the way. They long for coaching and training, and they deeply value the fact that they are making a significant contribution to the mission of the church.

Trainers are so busy getting people trained that when they leave a ministry there is always someone ready to take their place. They would regard it as a total failure if they left and no one was prepared to carry on the work they were doing. On the other hand, when those with ministry gifts leave, a hole is left in the ministry because no one steps in to take their place unless a trainer has been preparing someone for that role.

In churches that are strong in putting trainers in leadership roles and those with ministry gifts in ministry roles, the ministry continues to function even if someone moves away or a new church that attracts key people from the ministry of the parent church is started. No one suffers, because a trained person is always ready to step in at the right time. Churches need both trainers and those with ministry gifts. It is not a choice of one or the other, and God has so gifted the church that both exist in every church for the accomplishment of the mission of Christ.

What we have indicated here is that the discovery of one's basic ministry orientation—a trainer or a ministry performer—is more important than discovering one's actual gift in each orientation. Rarely does a person with ministry gifts function well in a trainer role. However, many times a trainer also does well in a ministry position. In order to be able to train others, the person really has to know how to function in that position. As a result, most ministry people know they are not trainers, but not all trainers realize so easily that they are primarily trainers.

In fact, trainers many times will enjoy doing ministry, but they will also want to get others involved in it. They will never be content just to do it themselves, and, ultimately, they gain their biggest satisfaction from the successes of the people they have trained. For example, I personally believe that God has gifted me as a trainer. Yet at times I enjoy doing ministry as well. However, I am usually in the process of training people while I am doing ministry, because that is my nature. For example, I conduct a full-scale public evangelistic meeting each year. I enjoy seeing the results of my labors, in people being baptized. This brings me great personal satisfaction. However, what thrills my heart even more is one of the people I have trained during the course of the meetings calling me up later and telling me how many people came to Christ because he or she held a series of meetings. This really excites me even more than seeing the people baptized from my work. That is the difference between a trainer and a ministry performer.

God's church today needs both groups of people operating in the church. When this happens, not only will the church function more smoothly, but people will be content and find satisfaction in their church positions because God has equipped them to serve in that role. Therefore, the first step in implementing a gift-based ministry approach is to make certain that those already in ministry are in their proper place in light of their gift orientation and that those who enter ministry in the future are assigned in harmony with this basic gift orientation.

Once this is understood and practiced, you can begin to build a structure that will support every member of your church in ministry. That will be the subject of our next chapter.

---

* Russell Burrill, *Revolution in the Church* (Fallbrook, Calif.: Hart Research Center, 1993), p. 99.

8

Creating an Organization to Support "Every-Member Ministry"

The organization of most churches makes it difficult for people to get involved in ministry. This is why gift-based ministry fails to happen in the vast majority of Adventist churches. The entire organization of the church is built around the premise that 20 percent of the people do 80 percent of the work. The plan of God is for all the people to be involved in ministry, yet most churches do not have the organizational grid work to support this idea.

Most Adventist churches are organized around a nominating committee meeting once a year (in some churches, every other year). The process is standard. You need the approval of the nominating committee to get into any ministry in the church because the church has made ministry involvement an elected position. In my book *Revolution in the Church* we suggested an alternate approach. Instead of the nominating committee nominating all the officers and ministry positions, the nominating committee would nominate only the officers; a lay ministry committee would appoint the ministry positions.

Many churches have tried this approach and found it workable. I have been told by many pastors and laypeople that this attempt to replace the process of election to ministry with appointment to ministry has worked well. It is now time to move beyond this initial step. People not only need to be placed in ministry rather than elected to ministry; they also need a support system in the church to help every-member ministry be effective.

A Ministry Philosophy of Every-Member Ministry

In order for every member to be involved in ministry, the church must have a basic philosophy of every-member ministry. This philosophy of ministry must be deeply ingrained in the very psyche of the church. It cannot be a philosophy that is accepted by only the pastor and a few members. It must permeate the entire church. It can never be assumed that the church members share this viewpoint. It must be constantly held up before them. The only one who can cast this vision for the church is the one perceived as the church leader.

In many cases the church leader is the pastor. In small churches it is often the matriarch or patriarch. If they do not buy into this vision, it will not happen. There are always those who think that they can bypass the leader and implement the new idea. It never works. This is why it is important that the main leadership of the church fully accept the concept. If you are reading this book because your church needs renewal, hopefully your leadership is already willing to do whatever it takes to turn the church around, including getting everyone into ministry.

You may be wondering why we are emphasizing the quality characteristic of gift-oriented ministry above the others. It is because we have discovered that in declining and plateaued churches it is this characteristic more than the others that will help turn the church around. Many of the other characteristics will improve as the church begins to get every member involved in ministry. So one of the first steps in church renewal is to work toward full acceptance of the every-member ministry philosophy. You may use my book *Revolution in the Church* as a study guide for prayer meeting or a discussion tool to use with the leadership. This is an excellent way to get people to buy into the concept of every-member ministry.

Once a philosophy of ministry is in place, the leadership must continually cast the vision for this kind of ministry. New people will continue to join the church, and they will need instruction on how this church operates. Older members need constant reminders that everyone is to be involved in ministry.

A Plan to Identify Ministry Opportunities

It is one thing to have a philosophy of lay ministry in place; it is another thing to move beyond the philosophy and actually have all the members involved in ministry. The first step in that process is to have in place a system that enables people to find a ministry in harmony with their spiritual gifts. A good church will have a sign-up list of opportunities readily available. Yet a church can never limit people to the list that the leadership has come up with. Leaders must always remember that the members themselves will come up with brand-new ministry opportunities, and the church must be ready to affirm people who choose a ministry outside of the norm. Churches need to have new ministry opportunities continually opening.

When new converts or newly transferred members join the church, there must be a way that the church can immediately orient them to its basic philosophy of ministry so that they quickly realize that all God's people are ministers. One way to accomplish this for new converts is through the laying on of hands at baptism, as discussed in *Revolution in the Church*.[1] Transferred members will need to attend an orientation class. This should be required of all who transfer. Otherwise, the church will become filled with new people who have not embraced the concept of every-member ministry. If this happens, it won't be long before the church is right back in the old situation of having a few members do all the work.

Part of this orientation process should include a chance for the leadership to get well acquainted with the new people and help them find a place of ministry in the body of Christ. Not only should time be taken to help them discover their basic gift orientation (trainer or ministry performer), but their individual spiritual gifts should be explored. In addition, their character, spiritual development, understanding of the Adventist message, and how well they relate to other people should be examined.

For example, a person who has just become an Adventist should not immediately be made a Sabbath school teacher in the senior division, even if their giftedness is in the area of teaching adults. Why? Because their doctrinal formation is still embryonic and they need time to embrace the Adventist message fully. However, you might place that person as an assistant teacher. The experienced teacher could then observe them and help them as they adjust. This would allow them to start using their giftedness in the correct way while under experienced teachers.

Once a person has been selected for a particular ministry, the person should then be invited to join that particular ministry. Notice that we suggest "invitation" rather than "recruitment." Recruitment carries too many negative connotations. Inviting someone to join assumes that the decision is up to the person—they have a choice.

How does the invitation to ministry happen currently in your church? Here is a typical scenario from an average Adventist church. After the nominating committee has agonized for weeks trying to find a Pathfinder leader, someone finally suggests Sister Rachel. Now, Sister Rachel has never served in Pathfinders or in children's Sabbath school, but we know that she is very sensitive and does whatever the church asks her to do. Knowing that this will be a "hard sell," the nominating committee insists that the pastor ask her to accept this position.

Arriving at Sister Rachel's home, the pastor comes quickly to the point. He tells her how the nominating committee has been struggling in an attempt to find a new Pathfinder leader. After much prayer the committee felt that the Lord was leading them to ask Sister Rachel to serve. He proceeds to tell her how certain he is that God is leading and that she will want to follow the leading of God in accepting this position. Of course, Sister Rachel does not want to disobey the leading of the Lord, so she accepts the position. The nominating committee breathes a sigh of relief, and the children suffer throughout the next year. And when it is all over, Sister Rachel leaves the church.

How much better it would be to go to Sister Rachel, offer her the position of Pathfinder leader, ask her to pray about it, and explain what the duties are and what skills are needed. Then leave it with her to pray it through and let the nominating committee know of her decision. The latter is the people-centered approach that is far superior to other methods, even if the church continues to use the nominating committee process.

The point to remember here is that you should not use high pressure to get people into ministry. You want people in a ministry in which they are comfortable, as well as in a position that God has equipped them to fill. Thus, the ultimate decision for ministry placement must be left with the people invited to serve; no one should ever be pushed into a ministry that they have not been gifted for or one that they have not prayed about before accepting.

Entering Ministry

So often when a new person enters an existing ministry there is no orientation to the background of the ministry. The church just assumes that the person already understands the ministry. New workers not only should be oriented but also need to understand how that particular ministry connects to the mission of the church. This assumes that the church has a clear mission that is understood by the members.

One of the ministry opportunities in a certain church is the need for someone to help wash dishes at the weekly potluck lunch that is held immediately after the worship service. This is about as unglamorous a ministry as you can have. It obviously needs someone with the spiritual gift of helps, but even then, people don't line up to wash dishes.

Let's suppose the ministry team approaches Brother Brown, who they know has the gift of helps. They wish to invite him to help them in their potluck ministry by doing dishes.

Instead of asking him to do dishes, the team leader instead invites him to be a part of the potluck ministry. He or she explains that the purpose of the weekly potluck is to provide a place where visitors are invited each Sabbath for a meal after the worship service. The purpose of this meal is to enable members to get better acquainted with the visitors and to socialize, so that hopefully many of those visitors will accept Jesus as their Savior and become members of the church. The potluck lunch makes this opportunity possible and thus is a vital link in reaching people for Jesus in your church.

Once Brother Brown sees how he can use his gifts in

such a meaningful ministry, he gladly accepts the responsibility, knowing that God is using his gifts in such a way that people will find Jesus. By connecting the ministry to the mission, the work becomes a ministry and not just a chore. This is probably the most important thing you can do as you bring people into a ministry, but it is something that is neglected most of the time by churches.

Another facet of bringing Brother Brown into this ministry is that he is not asked to perform a solo ministry—he is made a part of a ministry team. Jesus never invited people to do ministry all by themselves. Even the disciples were sent out two by two. Since the church is a community, even ministry should be done in community. (See my book *The Revolutionized Church of the 21st Century.*)

Such teams are not just task groups; they are holistic small groups. By turning your ministry groups into teams, you are also helping the church fulfill the other great need the church has—holistic small groups. In these groups there is accountability, nurture, and support. No one likes to feel that they are alone as they work for Jesus. They need to know that other members of their ministry team are supporting them on a regular basis.

The ministry team doesn't exist only to do potlucks; they also meet for worship and sharing times, thereby growing together spiritually in Christ as they go about the accomplishment of their ministry in providing potlucks so that new people can find Jesus.

When people are gifted in a specific area it doesn't mean that they can function without training. A regular training program needs to be utilized in the church for all people who enter ministry. Some ministries, such as dishwashing, will not need extensive training, but even a dishwasher needs to be trained to learn where things go and the process by which the dishes are cleaned.

Otherwise they are apt not to do it "right," and we end up criticizing them; they get discouraged and leave the ministry. This is why basic training for any ministry is an absolute necessity.

Keeping People in Ministry

Once people have become involved in a ministry, it does not mean the church's work and support for them are over. People need ongoing attention, or they will get discouraged and leave the ministry. Every-member ministry is something that is happening all the time in the church, and people need support for every stage of their ministry involvement. You might be thinking that this is a lot of work. It is, but the rewards are enormous as you see people becoming involved in the ministry of Christ. Actually, the creation and follow-through of this ministry support system is a ministry that someone in your church will need to embrace and make a reality.

One of the most important elements of keeping people in ministry is to ensure that they have been given generous doses of appreciation. One can never overdo the giving of thank-yous. Years ago a Sabbath school superintendent outdid herself with a special Sabbath school program. The next week I sent her a short thank-you note, expressing my appreciation for the excellent program. The next Sabbath she approached me and indicated that she had been working in that church for 25 years and had never been thanked before. How can we expect to keep people in a ministry if we don't take the time to let them know how much we appreciate their contribution to the ministry?

This does not mean just sending the perfunctory thank-you letter after every event, but instead, sending a special, handwritten word of thanks to people who go the second mile. When I worked with NET '98, one of the pastors at Pioneer Memorial church took the time to write a handwritten thank-you note to everyone who was involved in some kind of ministry with that program. With more than 1,000 volunteers, this was an awesome task, but one that was greatly appreciated by those involved. Such remembrances keep people going in ministry. It is not that they are working just to get noticed or receive a thank-you, but it is encouraging to know that one's contribution is noted and appreciated.

I mentioned that when people enter a ministry they need basic training for the ministry. However, it is also important for the church to provide ongoing training while people are engaged in meaningful ministry. Remember, you are investing in the whole person, and ongoing training is vital to their future development and involvement in other ministries of the church. So think through how your church can provide ongoing training events for your ministry personnel.

You may be wondering whether you have enough people to provide all these resources. You are just a small church, and you don't have the personnel to do it. Just remember, you are not alone in this. Your conference is there to support you. Most conferences have numerous training programs available, using either a person from the conference who will come to your church and provide the training or a video seminar to show to your workers. If your conference does not have this type of resource, they can refer you to places where you can purchase training videos. With the technology and resources of today, every Adventist church should be able to provide their members with the best training the Adventist Church has to offer.

Another aspect of supporting people in ministry is creating opportunities for those engaged in ministry to provide and receive regular feedback on their ministry involvement. This feedback should emerge from the ministry workers regarding what the church can do to help the ministry.

There also needs to be dialogue from the church to the workers as to how they can continually improve what they contribute to the ministry. This feedback should be both positive and negative. Don't wait until there is a problem to give feedback. Create an atmosphere in which this feedback is occurring on a regular basis. Remember, the goal is for people involved in ministry to grow spiritually so that they are truly discipled to become a people ready to meet Jesus when He comes. This is, above all else, our goal as Adventists. Ministry involvement is not merely to accomplish the tasks of the church; it is primarily a vehicle to ensure the spiritual growth of the members of the church.

Leaving Ministry

No one stays in a ministry forever, although some people think they are there from the cradle to the grave. People need transitions in their life—at times they are ready to move into new areas of ministry. No one should ever feel trapped in a ministry for the rest of his or her life. One of the reasons for ongoing training of those in ministry is so that they will develop new skills to serve Christ better in the future.

When people leave ministry, seldom do they give you the real reason for leaving. They will manufacture all kinds of excuses. Most churches simply accept the excuses and never find out exactly why the person is choosing to leave the ministry. So what are the real reasons that people leave ministry? I would suggest four: 1. They are looking for a new challenge and want to get involved in a new ministry. 2. They have been misplaced. They are a ministry performer, and they have been placed in a trainer role.

3. They have not been adequately trained, and so they feel unqualified for the present position. 4. They feel disqualified because of some sin in their life.

If the real reason is the last one, there is not much you can do except to minister to their spiritual needs and help them regain their spiritual life. Reason 1 is a challenge that is easy to address by getting them involved in the new ministry. Reasons 2 and 3 pose the greatest challenge and are important for the church to acknowledge. They would indicate that the church could do a better job of supporting or placing people in ministry. If a church does not discover these holes in its system, it will keep repeating the same mistakes and will not be able to keep people in ministry.

How can you learn the real reason for people wanting to get out of a ministry? The best way is for someone to do a personal interview with them. This interview should be conducted by a person who is neutral to the ministry so that the trust level is there. The ministry leader should never conduct this interview. The purpose of the visit is to learn the real reason that the person wishes to leave the ministry. This is not so that the ministry leader can be criticized, but so that the church can learn how to better serve people in that ministry in the future.

There should be no attempt to justify what the church or ministry leader did or did not do. The interviewer should create openness so that the person feels comfortable in sharing honestly. This will result in valid information that will keep the church from making the same mistakes twice. Sometimes it is impossible to conduct such an interview, because the person is unwilling. However, the church should do all it can to find out the reasons behind the exit from a particular ministry. This is an essential element in supporting people in ministry.

When people leave a ministry, they need to transition

into a new ministry. Noninvolvement is really not an option for the body of Christ. So when a person leaves one ministry, you begin the process all over again of looking at their spiritual gifts, their passions, their character, and their relational ability as you attempt to place them in another ministry.

Where to Begin

After reading this chapter, you may be feeling overwhelmed. You see why ministry involvement is not happening in your church. You know you desperately need a system-wide approach to every-member ministry, but there is so much to put in place for this to happen. Please do not be discouraged. Go back to the beginning of this chapter and take it step by step. You do not need to have the entire system in place before you begin. Add one part, and as that part is fully established, move on to the next. This chapter has simply given you the overview of a complete support system for every-member ministry.

Getting people into gift-based ministry is essential. It is one of the elements of a healthy church and correlates strongly with spiritual and numerical growth. I personally believe that it is impossible to restore a church to health and vitality without first restoring ministry to all the people of God. I have devoted two chapters in this book, and much additional material in my other books, to try clarifying the steps to implementing this characteristic because I believe it is such an essential part of restoring the church to health. Ellen White declared it clearly more than 100 years ago:

"The work of God in this earth can never be finished until the men and women comprising our church membership rally to the work, and unite their efforts with those of ministers and church officers." [2]

If we want to see the work finished and Jesus come,

then we as Adventists must return ministry to the people of God. Only when this happens can the work be finished and we can go home with Jesus. This is why every-member ministry is not an option for the Seventh-day Adventist Church. Why not discuss this now with your church leadership and begin to bring your church back to full vitality?

---

[1] Russell Burrill, *Revolution in the Church*, pp. 86-88.
[2] Ellen G. White, *Gospel Workers* (Washington, D.C.: Review and Herald Pub. Assn., 1948), p. 352.

9

Worship Him Who Made Heaven and Earth

A t the heart and center of Adventism is the call to worship the Creator. That call is enshrined in the most sacred of Adventist passages, the three angels' messages in Revelation 14. Yet in recent years nothing has so disturbed and disrupted Adventist churches as the subject of worship. Churches have been in conflict, split, and even destroyed over worship. That which should be a joy and a delight has become a cause of distress in many Adventist churches.

The problem lies in Adventist churches' attempting to copy the worship paradigms of other denominations. It is not that those paradigms are wrong; but when worship is developed not out of the congregation's need but through the imposing of an outside worship system on the congregation, then difficulties arise. Some people have felt that if they could just change the worship service, suddenly lost people would flock to the church, fulfilling the gospel commission. But this rarely happens.

The weekly worship service is meaningful only if hearts have been touched by God during the week. Otherwise it is just ornamental trimmings added to the church, and there is no vibrancy. Just changing the worship style without changing the hearts of the worshipers will do no good. Yet when people's hearts have been liberated by the good news of the gospel of Jesus, the worship service of such redeemed people will be vibrant, no matter what the style.

Bringing drums into the church, moving from choirs to worship teams, increasing the beat of the songs— these things do not create vibrancy. They are useless trimmings that create war in the church if the people have not been renewed first. Many of the things mentioned above might be utilized as part of the spiritual renewal occurring in churches, but the point here is that they must spring out of renewed hearts, not just be added in the hope that it will bring life. To do so is like tying green leaves to a dead tree. It may make the tree look vibrant at first, but within days the leaves rot, and the deadness looks disgusting.

Rather than focusing on merely changing the worship service, I have suggested in this book that vibrancy first be restored in other areas. If the characteristics of *holistic small groups* and *gift-oriented ministry* are low in the church, as well as *inspiring worship,* then the church should first seek to restore gift-oriented ministry and holistic small groups before it deals with worship renewal. This would apply even more if *passionate spirituality* is low in the church. Now, if everything else except inspiring worship is up, obviously you would then deal with worship issues.

What I am suggesting here is that when you are dealing with a plateaued and declining church, do not begin your renewal with worship renewal. It must spring forth as a result of other restorations. Otherwise you will split the church and kill it. The path for returning churches to vibrancy rarely begins with worship renewal. Yet the result of returning to vibrancy is worship renewal.

Music

The minute that worship renewal is brought up, someone immediately thinks we are talking about the introduction of rock music and loud rhythms into the church. Please do not make that association. Some churches may feel comfortable using this style of music; most Adventist churches do not. One can have worship renewal without resorting to these more controversial styles. Yet Adventism is big enough to affirm those who do use them as well as those who are uncomfortable using these louder styles of music. What we must have is mutual respect and toleration for personal tastes in the area of music.

Music has been an area of conflict in the church throughout its history. Every new style, every new instrument, that has been introduced has created division in the church and the new instrument labeled a tool of the devil. Yet eventually the instrument becomes accepted and sometimes even becomes the symbol of orthodoxy in music. As generations change, music styles invariably change in the church. In the next few pages I wish to share a brief history of the many changes in styles of music that have occurred in the church throughout the ages.

Music Through the Ages

Praising God through music has been a vital part of biblical worship from the very beginning. One of the earliest worship expressions is that provided in Exodus just after the amazing deliverance of the Israelites from Egyptian bondage. It was led by the prophet Miriam and was a spontaneous expression of praise to God for the remarkable deliverance at the Red Sea. Exodus 15 describes the events and the words of the song that was sung. We have no record of the music style, but the Bible does indicate that musical instruments were used, such as the timbrel (Ex. 15:20). Not only were percussion instruments used, but there was dancing as well. Religious dancing appears to be a vital part of Old Testament worship. Worship was not something reserved for the intellect alone; the whole body was used in praise to God.

Later, Temple worship was instituted. The book of Psalms appears to be the greatest collection of the hymns used in Temple worship. David's act of worship in bringing the ark of the covenant to Jerusalem to the special place he had prepared was a great time of celebration and joy.

"Then David spoke to the chiefs of the Levites to appoint their relatives the singers, with instruments of music, harps, lyres, loud-sounding cymbals, to raise sounds of joy" (1 Chron. 15:16).

It appears that the Old Testament worshipers felt comfortable utilizing all kinds of instruments and vocal arrangements for the worship of the great God that they served. They worshiped God with stringed instruments as well as loud-sounding cymbals (similar to modern percussion). They also employed religious dance in their worship. In fact, most of us would not be comfortable with the Old Testament culture of religious worship. The worshipers were very expressive as they communicated their inner joy at creating a Temple for the infinite God and experiencing His deliverance. These things so filled the worshipers with joy that the joy exploded in loud expressions of praise to God. Psalm 150 is an example of how they were instructed to worship this awesome God:

"Praise the Lord! Praise God in His sanctuary; praise Him in His mighty expanse. Praise Him for His mighty deeds; praise Him according to His excellent greatness. Praise Him with trumpet sound; praise Him with harp and lyre. Praise Him with timbrel and dancing; praise Him with stringed instruments and pipe. Praise Him with loud cymbals; praise Him with resounding cymbals. Let everything that has breath praise the Lord. Praise the Lord!" (Ps. 150:1-6).

Old Testament worship clearly emphasized that there was nothing that could not be used to praise God. Therefore, biblically speaking, there is no such thing as a forbidden instrument. All instruments and all people can praise God. In fact, the emphasis in this psalm appears to be on the percussion instruments, the very instruments that cause discomfort for so many of us today. We need to be careful of condemning what God has commanded, even if we are not comfortable with it.

Early Christian Music

Our knowledge of early Christian music is limited, as is knowledge of Old Testament music. The earliest Christians inherited their music from the Old Testament, and it consisted of psalms, hymns, and spiritual songs (Eph. 5:19; Col. 3:16). No hymns of the early church have survived. Whenever music was used, it was to be both emotional and cerebral (1 Cor. 14:15), encompassing the whole heart (Eph. 5:19; Col. 3:16).

New Testament worship consisted of music that was joyful, like the Old Testament worship. By the time of Christ, worship in Judaism had become the domain of the professional singers who performed in the Temple for the people.[1] The early Christian church evidently restored congregational singing.[2] In this era music was to be not just performed but an expression of the people's worship of God. Participation in worship became the New Testament norm.

The Middle Ages and the Reformation

The apostasy of the Middle Ages was not only in doctrine, but also in music. Once again music was relegated to the realm of the professional, along with ministry and other worship issues.[3] The people's job was to watch, not participate. Therefore much of the music produced for the church during this era was for the professional to perform rather than for the populace to sing. The style of music chosen was reflective of the era and drawn from the popular culture, such as operas and High Masses. What we today refer to as classical music is the music that was used by the church for its great performances during the Middle Ages.[4]

Classical music can be a wonderful expression of praise to God when beautifully performed by a choir or trained vocalist. However, we need to be careful not to form our opinion of correct church music based on the music used by the Catholic Church of the Middle Ages. We must remember that even here the church was in apostasy by restricting music to the professionals and forbidding popular music sung by the masses. The New Testament has clearly articulated participation as a vital part of music. Classical music is not wrong in itself, but if that is the only style of music we have in the church today, we would be out of harmony with the biblical revelation. To be biblical, we must have all the people of God praising God with their voices in worship. That never happens when the church limits itself to classical music.

The Reformation, led in large part by Martin Luther, restored not only such great biblical truths as justification by faith and the priesthood of all believers, but also church music to the multitudes. One of the great contributions of Luther was that he set the people singing.[5] He took simple German folk tunes, placed Christian words to them, and let the people sing. He removed classical music with its performance-only orientation and started the people singing tunes they could easily sing. The doctrine of the priesthood of all believers included restoring music to all the people of God.

Luther's great hymn "A Mighty Fortress Is Our God" is an example of Luther's restoration. He composed the tune from the folk music of the German taverns and put religious words to the music; it brought singing back into the church.[6] Interestingly, when the church went into apostasy it removed singing from the people, and when God sent revival He set the people singing once again. The songs of the cathedral were too difficult for the people to sing; by using common melodies, Luther made it easy for the people to sing.

Luther was greatly criticized by the musicians of his era because he allowed the people to sing in their own language and took secular songs and placed religious words to them and then sang them in church. They felt this was apostasy. Little did they realize that having only professionals singing classical music was really apostasy when compared to the New Testament example. Luther's music was much more in harmony with the New Testament than was the Catholic Church and its exclusive use of classical music. It should be noted that Luther also used professional singing with classical music in his services, and added congregational folk singing.[7]

John Calvin went even further than Luther in the reformation of church music.[8] Because the organ was the primary instrument of the Roman Church, Calvin removed the organ and all musical instruments. He removed all choirs and had all singing done without accompaniment.[9] He declared that only God's Word was worthy to be sung; thus all songs were either psalms or Scripture put to music.[10] The music these songs utilized was taken from French and German folk music. Critics referred to Calvin's music as the "Geneva jigs." Calvin, like Luther, used the popular music of his day and put scriptural words to it.[11]

German Pietism was a strong movement in the late seventeenth and early eighteenth centuries that called the church from its dry scholasticism and cold formalism to a new emphasis on personal study of the Scriptures and experiential religion of the heart. The Pietists rejected all art music in worship because of the operatic tendencies of the time. Johann Sebastian Bach was in constant conflict with the Pietists. Instead of using classical, chorale-type music such as Bach's, the Pietists set their simple music to dancelike tunes.[12] Again in this Reformation movement we see the church moving away from performance to participation in music by giving the people sacred songs put to popular secular tunes.

It was the English dissenters who first introduced hymns composed by human hand, without a scriptural text.[13] The greatest of these was Isaac Watts, the father of English hymnody, many of whose hymns are still sung in Adventist churches. These hymns received great opposition from the established church, which wished to stick to the Psalter. So even the great hymns of the church received opposition as this new style of worship was introduced.[14] Today we defend these hymns as our heritage but forget that they too received opposition upon entry.

A further development in religious music occurred with the ministry of the Wesley brothers, Charles and John. They introduced the evangelistic and invitational-type songs into the church. In predestinarian Calvinistic theology there was no room for evangelistic fervor, but Charles Wesley's insistence of "free will" made the evangelistic invitation very important. To set their words to music, the Wesleys resorted again to the popular music of their day, choosing music from the folk songs of German origin as well as some from operatic tunes of the day.[15] Thus Wesley demonstrated the principle begun by Luther of taking popular secular songs, placing religious words to them, and bringing them into the church as religious music.

Church composers have historically used the music of the era to convey the gospel truth to unbelievers in language they can understand. As time passes, the new song whose tune was originally composed from secular forms gains respectability as sacred music. But by the time this happens, the tune is no longer popular secular music. Then new religious music is written using updated secular music; it is opposed until its secular connotations are forgotten, and then it too becomes well established and accepted. The historical pattern is consistent.

This brief overview should make it clear that there are no inherently religious tunes. Most religious tunes follow the same path as secular tunes—it is the words that make them religious or secular. To insist that only "religious" music be used in the church would eliminate much of the music in the Adventist hymnals. This long-range perspective is needed when we attempt to criticize those today who are taking secular styles of music and placing religious words to them. They are only repeating what every generation of musicians has done—arranging music that allows people to sing praises to God in a culturally appropriate way for their generation.

American Music

Inasmuch as Adventism arose in nineteenth-century America, a quick overview of the music of that day would be appropriate. Like their predecessors, these early Adventists borrowed the popular tunes of the day, placed religious words to them, and created Adventist hymns.

Nineteenth-century America was the era of camp meeting revivals. The music in these revivals was greatly influenced by Black spirituals. Refrains were the most important part of camp meeting songs. In fact, many times musicians of this era would take a traditional hymn and add a refrain.[16]

Adventists had their beginnings during the era of the camp meetings and the revivalistic period of frontier America. Thus we would expect the early songs to reflect this heritage. That is exactly what early Adventist hymnists did. They took popular camp meeting-style songs and added Advent words to them to create the Advent hymn.

James White, who had been a Millerite preacher, would often enter a church service by walking down the aisle singing "You Will See Your Lord a-Coming," beating out the tune by thumping on his Bible. He continued this practice with many hymns, even into his later years.[17] We would almost consider that sacrilegious today, but that was the era, and James White clearly reflected his time in his choice of music style. Evidently early Millerites used music with a strong beat and even kept time by clapping or beating on their Bibles.

The gospel song was introduced in the 1840s with the same musical form as the camp meetings songs—catchy melody, simple harmony and rhythm, and the inevitable refrain. Some gospel songs were written in the style of Stephen Foster, composer of "My Old Kentucky Home." Common to all gospel songs is the refrain. Most gospel songs dealt with an individual's personal experience rather than being directed toward God or about God—the primary emphasis in the music was on personal experience.[18]

The gospel song was popularized by the Moody-Sankey revivals of the late nineteenth century. Sankey made the revival song a permanent part of church hymnody. Songs were written in contemporary language, so in Moody's day the idea of being saved or lost was often couched in nautical terms because much of the population was either involved in or fascinated by seafaring. The Civil War period even produced military-type songs such as "Hold the Fort."[19]

Critics of the gospel song complained that it was too emotional and too physical—appealing to the feet more than to the heart and mind.[20] However, we have seen that most of the music that serves the church today is this same kind of music—physical, with rhythm. From the dance rhythm of Luther, to the Geneva jigs of Calvin, to the camp meeting ditties of early America, to the gospel songs—much of Christian music is the type that causes people's bodies to move with the melody. Try singing "Onward, Christian Soldiers!" without moving your feet to the rhythm.

Added to this was the music of the Salvation Army, which brought in the big brass band with cornet, trombone, tuba, and cymbals. The band played on the street corner and then marched back to the meetinghouse giving a rousing rendition of "Are You Washed in the Blood of the Lamb?" Inside the building the big bass drum continued to be used during the invitational hymn. This was in Europe.[21] In America musicians added the "two-step," or "polka," gospel song and the "waltz" songs,[22] such as Charles Gabriel's "The Glory Song," an Adventist favorite.

In the early twentieth century a new instrument was introduced into the church—the piano. Before this time the piano was forbidden as a church instrument. It was traditionally reserved for the concert hall. But Charles Alexander found that he was better able to lead the livelier gospel songs if they were played on the piano rather than the organ. During this time Homer Rodeheaver and Billy Sunday continued the use of the gospel song but made it even more spirited.[23]

In the 1940s another innovation occurred with the introduction of the gospel chorus, including such songs as "Into My Heart." Over the next several decades the Billy Graham Crusades had a major influence on the songs Christians sang by utilizing such popular composers as John Peterson and Bill Gaither. As in all gospel music, this music also represented the thought patterns of the day. Utilizing language that reflected how people felt, they couched it in contemporary music. One style of music often used by some modern composers of gospel songs has been called "folk," or "country." While opposed in its beginnings, it is now widely accepted by most churches.[24]

Over the past couple decades a new form of music has been introduced, popularly called "praise songs." Like their predecessors, these songs received much opposition as they entered the church, although today they are widely accepted in most Adventist churches. In some respects they are a return to the form of the Reformation period when songs were mainly Scripture texts or psalms put to contemporary music. Praise choruses have been a turnaround from the songs of "human devisings" made popular by the gospel song. Instead, they point the believer upward to God. Rather than focusing on human experience, they focus instead on praising God.

These modern choruses are used two ways in Adventist churches. Some congregations play them utilizing a soft rock beat, while others utilize them without the rock beat yet with much more gusto than the more formal hymns of traditional Adventism. Each church will need to decide which form they are comfortable with in worshiping God.

What can we learn from this brief overview of music history? Simply put, there has been and continues to be a wide variety of music available for churches to use. We also learn that every new instrument has had trouble upon entry into the church, but ultimately becomes accepted. We must revert back to Scripture, particularly Psalm 150, to see clearly that all instruments can be used to praise God. What a strike we take against the devil when we take an instrument that he has corrupted by his usage and turn it around to praise God.

This is in harmony with the themes of Scripture. It should make us very cautious in criticizing those whose musical tastes are different from our own. We may not enjoy all styles, but we can bless those who worship in a different way than we do, rather than criticize differing musical tastes. To judge others and feel that those with different musical tastes are spiritually low is not only wrong theology but poor Christianity. God help us as we seek to improve our worship service and to be charitable to one another as we grow together in musical tolerance.

---

[1] Charles Etherington, *Protestant Worship Music* (New York: Holt, Rinehart and Winston, Inc., 1962), p. 15.

[2] Donald Hustad, *Jubilate! Church Music in the Evangelical Tradition* (Carol Stream, Ill.: Hope Pub. Co., 1981), pp. 88, 89.

[3] *Ibid.*, pp. 100, 104, 105.

[4] Etherington, p. 62.

[5] *Ibid.*, pp. 92, 93.

[6] Hustad, p. 108.

[7] Etherington, pp. 94, 95.

[8] Hustad, p. 114.

[9] *Ibid.*, p. 116.

[10] *Ibid.*

[11] Hustad, pp. 116, 134, and Etherington, pp. 97-103.

[12] Hustad, p. 125.

[13] *Ibid.*, p. 126.

[14] *Ibid.*

[15] *Ibid.*, pp. 126, 127.

[16] *Ibid.*, pp. 128, 129.

[17] William A. Spicer, *Pioneer Days of the Advent Movement, With Notes on Pioneer Workers and Early Experiences* (Washington, D.C.: Review and Herald Pub. Assn., 1941), pp. 145-147.

[18] Hustad, pp. 130, 131.

[19] *Ibid.*, pp. 132, 133.

[20] *Ibid.*, p. 134.

[21] *Ibid.*

[22] *Ibid.*
[23] *Ibid.*, p. 136.
[24] *Ibid.*, p. 139.

10

How Do We Worship?

In the previous chapter we explored the tremendous heritage we have in Christian music. We also discovered that the church in its apostasy reverted to performance music rather than participatory music. Every great revival set the people singing by adding religious words to contemporary music styles taken from the secular world. Our generation is simply following the pattern of all other great revivals of the past. The new music is initially opposed, but eventually it becomes accepted.

Should the church keep changing its musical style and way of worship to reflect the modern culture? All churches keep changing, whether they realize it or not. Our world is vastly different from what it was a few years ago. Methods that worked in the past do not necessarily work now. Failing to change in view of the changing situation in our world is to invite death to the church, finding ourselves keepers of the aquarium instead of fishers of men. Why don't we just preserve the past? Are we really satisfied with the past? Sometimes we forget that the Adventist Church in North America has been in Laodicean slumber. Something must happen to wake it up. Yet there are many who are afraid of an awakened, praying church. Thus they do all in their power to keep it asleep.

On January 31, 1829, when Martin Van Buren was governor of New York, he wrote a letter to President Andrew Jackson. Notice how natural it is to resist change:

"The canal system of this country is being threatened by the spread of a new form of transportation known as railroads. The federal government must preserve the canals for the following reasons.

"One, if boats are supplanted by railroads, serious unemployment will result. Captains, cooks, drivers, hostlers, repairmen, and lock tenders will be left without means of livelihood, not to mention the numerous farmers now employed in growing hay for horses.

"Two, boat builders would suffer, and towline, whip, and harness makers would be left destitute.

"Three, canal boats are absolutely essential to the defense of the United States. In the event of the expected trouble with England, the Erie Canal would be the only means by which we could ever move the supplies so vital to waging modern war.

"As you may well know, Mr. President, railroad carriages are pulled at the enormous speed of 15 miles per hour by engines that, in addition to endangering life and limb of passengers, roar and snort their way through the countryside, setting fire to crops, scaring the livestock, and frightening women and children. The Almighty certainly never intended that people should travel at such breakneck speed."[1]

In a multicultural society such as North America today, change is inevitable. Yet differing cultural practices are dividing churches. Rather than affirm our cultural differences, we make the mistake of declaring that our cultural practice is in harmony with Scripture and, therefore, all others are not. Such an attitude is unfortunate. There are no superior cultures. All cultures are fallen, including my own. God has incarnated Himself in all fallen cultures. Amazingly, this mighty God allows us to worship Him in ways that are most meaningful to the worshiper, in harmony with their culture.

Differing cultural practices exist in worship around the world, but the reality is that the world has now come to North America, bringing to light the multicultural variations. For example, in Micronesia people must remove their shoes when entering a church, while in the Caribbean women are required to wear a hat to church. In African churches worship involves rhythmic body movement and clapping.

Indigenous North American cultures display their own differences. African-American churches may dialogue a little with the preacher ("Amen," "Preach it, brother," etc.), while in many Anglo-North American churches one is expected to be totally silent. Can you imagine people from all these cultures worshiping together in the same church each Sabbath? Yet this is reality in many urban Adventist churches today. We need to be careful not to criticize differing cultural approaches. Instead, we need to reexamine our worship practices and become more culturally attuned. While we may not want to follow the cultural practices of other groups in our church, if we are sincere Christians we will not criticize people whose tastes in worship are different from ours.

Music and the Changing Culture

In no one area do these changing cultures clash more than in the area of music. In the previous chapter we discovered that every new generation seems to bring with it a new form of music. When I first entered ministry, I was taught that the gospel song was a bad style of music and should not be used in divine worship. In the syllabus for my church music class was the following quotation:

"Almost any examination of text and music is bound to reveal a serious mismating. These tunes, these low-class earthly fellows, are married to the wrong girls. . . . If, for example, you are a placid and normally cheerful tune, it must be difficult to be your smiling self if your wife is constantly at your elbow with the depressing query, 'Shall We Gather at the River?' . . . Gospel hymns represent, as I have said, connubial misfits, and this is undoubtedly one of the reasons why time has to a great extent expunged them. They still hold a nostalgic place in the affections of a vanishing generation, but in the services of enlightened churches they are never heard."[2] But today we defend the gospel song and attempt to forbid newer forms of musical expression. The perspective of history is helpful in understanding some of the present quarrels engulfing many Adventist churches regarding music.

I acknowledge that there are some forms of music that should be given much thought before utilizing them. Rock music, because of its strong secular connotations, may be difficult to utilize in Adventist churches. Likewise, some music written in a minor key might need to be questioned. Some minor keys may have the tendency to depress some people. If the minor-key prelude music played at the beginning of the church service depresses some people, it may take the rest of the service to build them back up. While this kind of minor-key music is not wrong to use, it may be inappropriate if we are trying to create a happy, joyful feeling in worship.[3] Our music could be creating a sad, depressed feeling, totally incompatible with Christian worship.

"Those who make singing a part of divine worship should select hymns with music appropriate to the occasion, not funeral notes, but cheerful, yet solemn, melodies."[4]

"Let us with reverent joy come before our Creator,

with 'thanksgiving, and the voice of melody.' " [5]

"The hour for joyful, happy songs of praise to God and His dear Son had come." [6]

Participatory worship was a major characteristic of both early Christian and Reformation times. Middle Ages Romanism removed music from the congregation and put it in the hands of the professional. If we are truly Protestant and believe in the priesthood of all believers, we must not let our church service become a professional musical program and call it worship. We must let all the people of God praise Him in song.

"The singing should not be done by a few only. All present should be encouraged to join in the song service. . . . There are times when a special message is borne by one singing alone or by several uniting in song. But the singing is seldom to be done by a few." [7]

Like the music style of the church, every kind of musical instrument has been condemned as unfit for the church, including the piano, organ, guitar, drum, etc. However, we have discovered from Scripture that there are no evil instruments. All musical instruments can be used in the praise of our awesome God. The problem with instruments has more to do with how they are played than with the instrument itself. Psalm 150 makes it clear that all musical instruments are fit to be used in praise to God; the passage especially mentions the percussion instruments. We must be careful we do not condemn what God condones.

Those who condemn some instruments today would be shocked by biblical worship. Our style of worship varies greatly from the limited understanding we have of New Testament worship. Ellen White herself strongly endorses the usage of all kinds of musical instruments in Adventist worship.

"Let the talent of singing be brought into the work.

The use of musical instruments is not at all objectionable. They were used in religious services in ancient times. The worshipers praised God upon the harp and cymbal, and music should have its place in our services. It will add to the interest."[8]

"I am glad to hear the musical instruments that you have here. God wants us to have them."[9]

There is only one reference to guitars in the writings of Ellen White, and it is a positive one.[10] There is also only one major reference to drums, and it is negative. However, in honesty, one must examine the context. One discovers that Ellen White is condemning not the instrument but the emotional excitement that was created and that resulted in the holy flesh offshoot in Indiana. Note the statement:

"It is impossible to estimate too largely the work that the Lord will accomplish through His proposed vessels in carrying out His mind and purpose. The things you have described as taking place in Indiana, the Lord has shown me would take place just before the close of probation. Every uncouth thing will be demonstrated. There will be shouting, with drums, music, and dancing. The senses of rational beings will become so confused that they cannot be trusted to make right decisions. And this is called the moving of the Holy Spirit."[11]

Upon analysis, one can easily see that Ellen White is condemning the bedlam of noise, not the instruments. To utilize this statement to declare that Ellen White is opposed to drums is not fair to her. She did not say that. Using such logic, one would have to assume that Ellen White also opposed music, since it is listed next to drums. That is obviously not true, so we need to make certain we are viewing her writings in context.

Ellen White did give strong instruction on how Adventists were to conduct song services. She was concerned that they be done well. Her counsel seems to suggest the worship team concept that many modern Adventist churches are utilizing.

"Another matter which should receive attention, both at our camp meetings and elsewhere, is that of singing. . . . Organize a company of the best singers, whose voices can lead the congregation, and then let all who will, unite with them. . . . They should devote some time to practice, that they may employ this talent to the glory of God." [12]

"In the meetings held, let a number be chosen to take part in the song service. And let the singing be accompanied with musical instruments skillfully handled. We are not to oppose the use of instruments of music in our work. This part of the service is to be carefully conducted, for it is the praise of God in song. The singing is not always to be done by a few. As often as possible, let the entire congregation join." [13]

Early Adventist worship was unrestricted. They met in homes and barns, virtually any place that could hold them. They did not have formal religious services. Their meetings were more like modern-day small groups. They met for Bible study and social meetings. [14] The worship was highly participative, with much time for testimonies and prayer. It was not liturgical at all. The power of God was freely displayed in these services and even resembled what is called Pentecostalism today.

"The Lord worked in mighty power setting the truth home to their hearts. Sister Durben knew what the power of the Lord was, for she had felt it many times, and a short time after I fell she was struck down, and fell to the floor, crying to God to have mercy on her. When I came out of vision, my ears were saluted with Sister Durben's singing and shouting with a loud voice." [15] "Singing, I saw, often drove away the enemy and shouting would beat him back." [16]

"The spirit came and we had a powerful season. Brother and Sister Ralph were both laid prostrate and remained helpless for some time." [17]

"The power of God descended something as it did on the day of Pentecost, and five or six who had been deceived and led into error and fanaticism fell prostrate to the floor." [18]

Most of us would feel very uncomfortable with early Adventist services. The early Adventists thought they had escaped the formalism of other churches, but now we have brought formalism into our services, and the lively, exciting, powerful, Spirit-filled services of early Adventism sound like Pentecostalism to us.

How did Adventists lose their exciting worship services? At the turn from the nineteenth century to the twentieth, fanaticism broke out in Adventist circles. This was the time in the rest of the Christian world that Pentecostalism was emerging, and Adventism was not unaffected. Led by A. T. Jones,[19] the Adventist holiness movement paralleled that in the Christian world. Its ultimate expression was found in the holy flesh movement in Indiana, referred to when we discussed drums.[20] Rank Pentecostalism had broken out in Adventist ranks.

Pentecostalism was frowned upon in most of the Christian world at this time, and mainline Adventists also spurned it. Adventists wished to divorce themselves from these extremes. This moved the Adventist Church away from the extremes of the early days and more into line with worship in mainstream Protestantism. In fact, there appeared to be an attempt to bring Adventist worship into line with other evangelical Christian denominations. Thus we started copying the worship services of the more liturgical churches, and although we never became as formal as some of them, we departed a long way from our roots. Tragically, our movement in worship toward formalism brought us problems similar to those of mainline denominations, where half of the membership does not even attend worship.

Ellen White counseled the church to avoid both extremes, Pentecostalism and formalism, but it is hard to remain balanced.

"God is displeased with your lifeless manner in His house, your sleepy, indifferent ways of conducting religious worship. You need to bear in mind that you attend divine service to meet with God, to be refreshed, comforted, blessed, not to do a duty imposed upon you."[21]

"The evil of formal worship cannot be too strongly depicted, but no words can properly set forth the deep blessedness of genuine worship."[22]

"The things you have described as taking place in Indiana, the Lord has shown me would take place just before the close of probation. Every uncouth thing will be demonstrated."[23]

Clapping and Hand Raising

As cultures have mingled together in North America, it has become more common to experience clapping and hand raising in Adventist churches. This form of worship was virtually absent from Anglo Adventist churches in North America back in the 1950s, but it is common today. Some feel it is wrong. In one church I was visiting I opened a bulletin that stated that saying amen in worship is reverent, but clapping is irreverent. Is this true?

Interestingly, there are no biblical texts advocating that we should shout "Amen" if we agree with something, although biblical people would use the amen ("let it be so") at the conclusion of prayers or hymns. Only Psalm 47:1 mentions clapping: "O clap your hands, all peoples; shout to God with the voice of joy."

Evidently we do have a command in Scripture to clap

our hands in praise to God. Admittedly it is only one text, but it is in the context of worship. Therefore we must be careful to prohibit what God has commanded. Some have suggested that saying "Amen" means you are praising God, but clapping indicates you are applauding the person. That, of course, is total nonsense. Have you ever noticed that some people get louder amens than others? So let us be careful not to invent theories that, upon examination, are totally unfounded.

Ellen White refers to clapping only one time. She was speaking at the Groveland, Massachusetts, camp meeting to more than 15,000 people. As she spoke she was interrupted by applause several times. Evidently she had no problem with people interrupting her sermon with applause.

"I was stopped several times with clapping of hands and stomping of feet. I never had a more signal victory." [24]

There are nine Bible references to hand raising, all of them advocating it (Ps. 28:2; 63:4; 119:48; 134:2; 141:2; Lam. 2:19; 3:41; Neh. 8:6; and 1 Tim. 2:8). This is strong evidence in both Testaments. Note the one New Testament reference:

"Therefore I want the men in every place to pray, lifting up holy hands, without wrath and dissension" (1 Tim. 2:8).

Ellen White refers positively to Solomon raising his hands to God as he prayed. She also indicates doing so herself, and even infers that she would be pleased if every ambassador for Christ would do so in pointing people to Jesus. [25] There can be no question that hand raising is a biblical practice with wide support in Scripture and in the writings of Ellen White.

However, it probably was the cultural way that people in Bible times prayed, as well as in Ellen White's time. This does not mean we always have to pray raising our hands, but it also means we cannot forbid it. To do so would stand in direct contradiction to Scripture, as well as Ellen White, a stand no Adventist can support. I may not be comfortable with hand-raising, so I may not wish to participate, but I should not hold back those who feel compelled by the Spirit to worship God in this demonstrable way.

Conclusion

I have chosen to devote these final two chapters to worship. Why? Because it is probably the biggest obstacle in renewing dead and dying churches. They wish to cling to their dead worship form and criticize anything new. I have written this, not to advocate any extremes, but to create openness to new forms of worship that are more in harmony with our roots than the formalism to which conventional Adventism in the twenty-first century has become accustomed. I hope the word "balance" is heard as these chapters are read.

Furthermore, I have written these chapters because, as I stated when I began this discussion, a mistake is made when we attempt to transform the worship service without first transforming the hearts of the people. In addition, I feel strongly that a restoration of holistic small groups and gift-based ministry must precede any attempt to revitalize worship. Once these are in place, worship revitalization will come naturally.

Most churches have chosen the opposite approach and tried to begin revitalization by renewing worship. This is a Band-Aid approach and does not work. People do not come flocking to Adventist churches simply because they have revised their worship services. Deep, spiritual renewal must occur first. This is what will draw people to the church.

Revitalization! What a need! O how we long for it to

happen in our churches. It is my hope that this book will help your church begin the exciting process of becoming a vibrant agency for God in these last days. May God restore you to vibrancy once again. Remember, however, that there can be no forward movement in this direction without much prayer. Revitalization is a work of the Holy Spirit and not of human devising. This is why prayer is so crucial to the revitalization movement.

Remember the process: 1. Pray. 2. Re-create the dream. 3. Analyze where you are through natural church development. 4. Work on your minimum factors. 5. Restore holistic small groups and gift-based ministry. 6. Let a revitalized worship occur. 7. Pray.

Actually, prayer must be a vital part of the entire process. I have placed it at the beginning and the end, but it must occur throughout the revitalization process. To awaken the dead takes the power of the Holy Spirit. Latch hold of it now and let the Spirit change your church and bring it back to vibrancy, health, and the fulfillment of God's great mission.

---

[1] David Newman, "Changes at *Ministry*," *Ministry*, January 1991 (quotation cited from letter to Andrew Jackson), p. 5.

[2] Archibald Davison, *Church Music, Illusion and Reality* (Cambridge, Mass.: Harvard University Press, 1952), pp. 113, 114, quoted in Harold B. Hannum, *Church Music Syllabus*.

[3] Etherington, *Protestant Worship Music*, p. 213.

[4] Ellen G. White, *The Voice in Speech and Song* (Boise, Idaho: Pacific Press Pub. Assn., 1988), p. 434.

[5] Ellen G. White, *Lift Him Up* (Hagerstown, Md.: Review and Herald Pub. Assn., 1988), p. 254.

[6] Ellen G. White, *The Spirit of Prophecy* (Battle Creek, Mich.: Seventh-day Adventist Pub. Assn., 1870), vol. 1, p. 28.

[7] Ellen G. White, *Counsels on Health* (Mountain View, Calif.: Pacific Press Pub. Assn., 1957), p. 481.

[8] Ellen G. White, *Evangelism* (Washington, D.C.: Review and Herald Pub. Assn., 1970), pp. 500, 501.

[9] *Ibid.*, p. 503.

[10] Ellen G. White, in *Historical Sketches of the Foreign Missions of*

the Seventh-day Adventists (Basle: Imprimerie Polyglotte, 1886), p. 195.

[11] Ellen G. White, *Selected Messages* (Washington, D.C.: Review and Herald Pub. Assn., 1958), book 2, p. 36.

[12] White, *The Voice in Speech and Song,* p. 434.

[13] White, *Gospel Workers,* pp. 357, 358.

[14] For further information on the early Adventist social meeting, see Russell Burrill, *The Revolutionized Church of the 21st Century.*

[15] Ellen G. White, *Manuscript Releases* (Silver Spring, Md.: Ellen G. White Estate, 1990), vol. 5, p. 98.

[16] *Ibid.,* p. 238.

[17] *Ibid.,* vol. 4, p. 323.

[18] Arthur L. White, *Ellen G. White: The Early Years* (Washington, D.C.: Review and Herald Pub. Assn., 1985), vol. 1, p. 169.

[19] This is the same A. T. Jones who led out in the 1888 movement on righteousness by faith. At this time, however, he had moved into apostasy. Jones eventually left the Adventist Church and joined a Sabbathkeeping Pentecostal body.

[20] It should be noted that Jones did not approve of the holy flesh movement and its extremes in Indiana, even though he had tendencies in those directions.

[21] Ellen G. White, "The New Heart," *Review and Herald,* Apr. 14, 1885.

[22] E. G. White, *Gospel Workers,* p. 357.

[23] E. G. White, *The Voice in Speech and Song,* p. 417.

[24] Arthur L. White, *Ellen G. White: The Lonely Years* (Washington, D.C.: Review and Herald Pub. Assn., 1984), vol. 3, p. 46.

[25] See Ellen G. White, *Prophets and Kings* (Mountain View, Calif.: Pacific Press Pub. Assn., 1917), p. 40; "Christ Gives Repentance," *Signs of the Times,* Aug. 18, 1890.

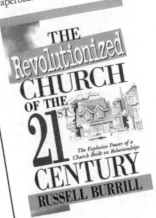

TT

**FACE TO FACE
WITH JESUS
BIBLE STUDY GUIDES**

These study guides
introduce people
to who Jesus is; why
He came to earth;
His ministry, message,
and death; and the
promise of His
soon return.
By Kurt Johnson.
0-8280-1362-4.
US$4.99, Can$7.49.

**LESSONS FROM THE
LIFE OF NEHEMIAH
BIBLE STUDY GUIDES**

An easy-to-use Bible
study guide on the
life of Nehemiah.
By Ellen White.
0-8280-1437-X.
US$4.99, Can$7.49.

**LIFELINE BIBLE STUDY
GUIDES, BOOKS 1 AND 2**

Key doctrines of the Bible
in an easy-to-use format.
By Kurt Johnson.
Book 1: 0-8280-0974-0.
US$4.99, Can$7.49.
Book 2: 0-8280-0975-9.
US$3.99, Can$5.99.

Study Guides
for Small Groups

Ways to Shop

- Visit your local Adventist Book Center®
- 1-800-765-6955
- www.AdventistBookCenter.com

REVIEW AND HERALD®
PUBLISHING ASSOCIATION
HELPING OTHERS PREPARE FOR ETERNITY

Price, and availability subject to change. Add GST in Canada.